THE MASTER BOOK OF ESCAPES

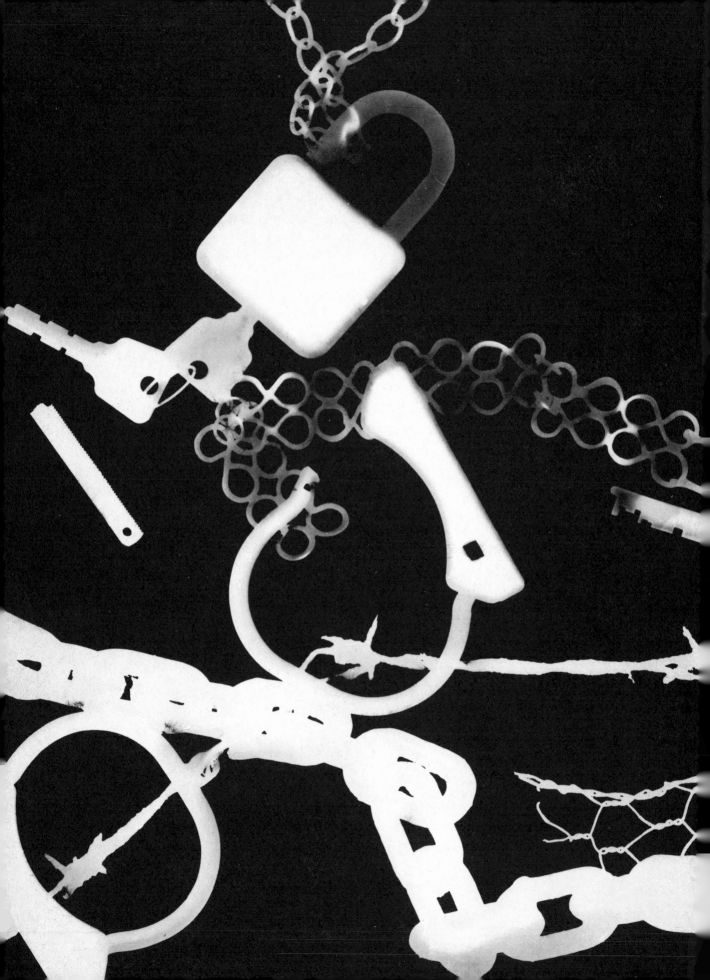

WRITTEN AND ADVISED BY

Donald McCormick

WITH A FOREWORD BY AIREY NEAVE
A leading organiser of underground escape lines
in North-West Europe: 1940/45

The Master Book of Escapes

the world of escapes and escapists
from Houdini to Colditz
keys, locks and chains
rafts, jungles and prisons
survival against all the odds

Franklin Watts, Inc. · New York · 1975

First published in 1974 in Great Britain
by Hodder Causton Ltd.
First American publication 1975
by Franklin Watts, Inc.

Copyright © 1974 by Hodder Causton Ltd.
SBN: 531-02801-1.
Library of Congress Catalog Card Number: 74-10347
Printed in Great Britain
by Sir Joseph Causton & Sons Ltd.

Contents

Foreword

Donald McCormick is right. It takes all kinds to make a successful escaper. (You may prefer 'escapist', which sounds more professional.) They have very different backgrounds and personalities. Few human beings are tested in this way, and no one can foresee how they will turn out. In my experience it is the modest and practical person who survives. The James Bonds of this world are too obvious. So are the big talkers. Poon Lim knew how to catch and dry fish at sea, and he did not lose his head.

However you define it, escape is seldom completely impossible. It is imagination and the capacity to seize the opportunity which count. Much depends on your physical and moral state. You cannot succeed without meticulous detail. Many rot in prison or are executed, because they are unprepared. During my escape from Colditz in 1942, I made an extraordinary mistake. I ate a large bar of chocolate in a station waiting room. I should have known that ordinary Germans had been deprived of chocolate for years by war-time controls.

When I was young, I was obsessed by the escape of Winston Churchill. I read all the escape books of the First World War. Many escapes are imitations of those which have gone before. The example of the men and women who get through has often led others to succeed. Never say it could not happen to you, for we still live in a dangerous world. By reading this fascinating book, you may derive inspiration, should you ever be put to the test.

AIREY NEAVE

Chapter 1

It takes all kinds...

Escape is not a simple word to define. It means many different things to many people. It covers a wide and sometimes unexpected range of subjects and activities. It is an act which may call for courage, patience, determination, a variety of skills and imagination; it can equally be caused by cowardice, lack of patience, inability to cope with life and sheer impulse.

And just to make things more complicated, sometimes, though not often, the act of escape can turn the coward into a hero and rescue the individual from the very despair that holds him back in life.

It takes all kinds to make a successful escapist. One of the most remarkable escapers of all time actually made a living out of it by turning escapology into an art. His real name was Ehrich Weiss, who later became renowned as one of the highest-earning music hall artistes of all times. Harry Houdini.

This naturalised American citizen was such a genius in the craft of escaping from seemingly impossible situations that during his life-time many people were convinced there was something super-human, or even super-natural about him.

Sir Arthur Conan Doyle, the creator of Sherlock Holmes and a keen student of spiritualism, was convinced that Houdini was a medium and that his feats could only be explained in this way. The President of the British College of Psychic Medicine, J. Hewatt McKenzie, went further than this. He alleged that Houdini 'dematerialised his body and oozed out.'

In fact Houdini's escaping talents were the result of a keen brain, tremendous concentration, years of study and patience in learning how to escape. He once said that he owed every-thing to his wife, that she brought him luck and that before he married her he had never achieved anything worthwhile.

We shall take a look again at Houdini later. Meanwhile it is worth recording that he lived from 1874 until 1926, that he

**Houdini: The greatest
escapist of all time**

staged underwater escapes from locked, roped and weighted wooden containers while he himself had hands and feet shackled.

Two of his most sensational stunts were never staged, though one can be sure that, having put them forward, he had thought out every detail: one was to escape when handcuffed to a parachute to be dropped from New York's Woolworth Building, the other was to escape from a nailed barrel in which he was to be swept over Niagara Falls.

No wonder Houdini was regarded by audiences as something of a wizard and that he was invited to become a member of the American Society of Magicians.

But few people are as lucky as Houdini in that they are able to turn escapology into a profession. Generally speaking, we think of the act of escape as an heroic effort to break out of some form of imprisonment, or to get away from a desert island, jungle or the Sahara Desert.

Houdini in the casket just before it was submerged: he stayed under water for 1½ hours

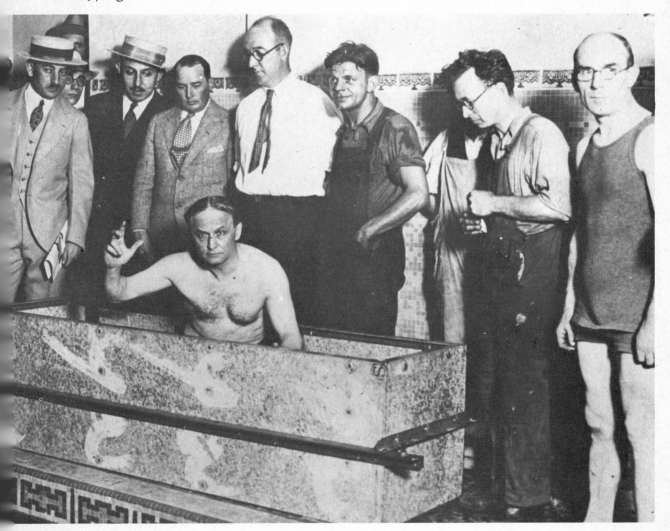

It will be mainly with these two types of escape that this book will concern itself. But at the outset it is just as well to mention some of the types of escape. The act itself can epitomise the heights of courage, or the depths of despair. The youth seeking to turn his back on the world and become a priest or monk is in a sense a virtuous escapist. Yet wisely the Church gives him some years in which to make up his mind whether he merely wants to escape from the world and responsibility or to escape *into* a world where he can serve his fellow-beings. Then again, at the other extreme, the would-be suicide is also an escapist, the worst kind of all in that he seeks to opt out of life completely.

Strangely we often sympathise with the escaper, even though he may be a criminal. And, while we should be on the side of law and order, sometimes it turns out that the person who escapes from prison, does so solely to prove his innocence. Not often, perhaps, but there are some very good examples of this.

Take the case of Alfred Hinds. He escaped from prison four times – three times during a twelve-year period in jail – in attempts to prove his innocence. Born in Britain in 1917, Hinds' first escape was from a Borstal institution for juvenile offenders in 1939 and he remained free for five months. Then in December, 1953, Hinds was sentenced at the Old Bailey in London to twelve months' preventive detention for having taken part in a £38,000 raid on Maple's stores in Tottenham Court Road, an offence of which he always insisted he was innocent.

In November 1955, Hinds escaped from Nottingham Prison and evaded arrest until eight months later when he was captured in Dublin and sent back to Britain, this time to Pentonville Prison. During this eight-month period he bought a cottage at the seaside town of Greystones, County Wicklow, 25 miles from Dublin, where he lived under the alias of Patrick Joseph Flynn.

In March, 1957, Hinds argued his own case at Nottingham Assizes, for escaping from lawful custody at Nottingham and was acquitted of the charge of breaking out of prison, but given an 11-day sentence on the lesser charge of escaping from custody. In May of that year he appealed to the Court of Criminal Appeal against this conviction, but his appeal was dismissed.

On 24 June, 1957, Hinds again escaped, this time from the Law Courts in the Strand, where he was due to appear in court at 10.30 am in an action listed as 'Hinds versus the Prison Commissioners', but he was recaptured five and a half hours later as he was trying to get away by plane to Dublin from Lulsgate Airport, Bristol.

His attempt at a getaway on this occasion was ingenious. Hinds' own account of it was that he had been to the Law

**Alfred Hinds in France
during one of his escapes**

Courts on three previous occasions and therefore had had
ample opportunity of considering the best means of escaping,
'bearing in mind that I did not want to commit violence of
any sort.'

On one of these occasions he had noticed that the prison
officers always used a staff canteen and went to a certain
lavatory. If he could obtain a key to that lavatory, he thought
he could lock his escorts in and escape.

Hinds discussed his escape plan with a prisoner about to be
discharged from Pentonville – 'a notorious locksmith' –
who agreed to leave a key to the lavatory under a specified
table in the staff canteen at the Law Courts. When Hinds
arrived at the Law Courts he had to assure his prison
officer escorts that it was 'normal procedure' to go to the staff
canteen.

He succeeded and found a parcel stuck under the table with
adhesive tape. But instead of the expected key he found a
small parcel with a padlock and two keys.

13

'That was quite a shock,' said Hinds afterwards, and he
added, 'I knew some alternative arrangement must have been
made.'

Hinds, always quick-witted, realised what that arrangement
must be when he got to the lavatory. There were two screw
eyes – one on the door and one on the jamb.

'Their absolute newness and glaring chrome startled me,'
said Hinds. 'I realised that something must be done
immediately because they were so obvious.'

When he had asked to go to the lavatory his handcuffs had
been removed. He had been escorted there by two warders.
He had the padlock hidden under a mackintosh over his right
arm. When he got to the lavatory door, he held the door open
and bowed the officers inside. One went through, but the
other seemed suspicious.

'So I pushed him inside,' said Hinds, 'pulled the door to
and locked it with the padlock. I walked right through the
"Bear Garden" (a large waiting-hall for solicitors, solicitors'
clerks and clients) as fast as discretion would allow me, out
into the Strand, and then went to the Temple tube station.'

Eventually he was driven by car to the airport at Bristol,
110 miles distant, where he booked a single ticket in the name
of Cottrell to Dublin, but neglected to pick up the three
pounds change due to him for the two five-pound notes he
had tendered.

This minor slip on his part drew the attention of the BEA
receptionist who, noticing his nervousness, checked his
resemblance to the description of the escaped prisoner which
had been circulated. The police were telephoned, the plane's
departure was delayed and Hinds was once again arrested.
Yet, when on 11 July, 1957, Albert James Hinds, Alfred's
brother, and Anthony John Maffia were charged jointly with
unlawfully aiding Hinds' escape from prison, Miss Reed, the
27-years-old receptionist who had spotted Hinds, told the
judge that she admired Hinds and regretted having recognised
him.

So Alfred Hinds once more returned to prison and then on
1 June, 1958, less than a year after his last escape, he once
more made a bid for freedom, this time from Chelmsford Jail.
He succeeded, with the aid of a fellow prisoner, by scaling a
20-foot wall and being picked up by a waiting car. Again he
went to Dublin, where he set up a car business under an
assumed name and remained at liberty for twenty months
while the police searched the whole of Europe for him.
Eventually he was re-arrested in early 1960.

In the end, despite all these set-backs, Hinds triumphed.
In 1964 he proved his innocence by winning a libel action
against former Detective Chief Superintendent Herbert
Sparks, the man who had arrested him for the original
robbery. Sparks had written a newspaper article saying that

Chelmsford Jail: Hinds escaped over the wall on the right

Hinds was guilty of the robbery. The High Court awarded Hinds £1,300 damages plus court costs after Hinds had served the bulk of his twelve years' sentence in prison or on the run. Hinds later appealed to the House of Lords where he was the first person ever to conduct his own case, without solicitors, against the Appeal Committee.

For sheer determination and patience Alfred Hinds rivalled even Robert the Bruce in his efforts to emulate the persevering spider.

**Re-arrested again, but for
the last time**

General Giraud

Thus there are several different types of escapist and it goes without saying that there are just as many different character types who make successful escapers. Probably the only single quality each of these types of escapers has in common with the rest is that of determination and a certain amount of ruthlessness. Sadly, this applies as much to the would-be suicide as to the prisoner-of-war scaling the jail walls.

But determination and ruthlessness alone are not enough. Many have the will to escape, but lack the know-how and today escape is not merely an art requiring sometimes much technical knowledge, but almost a profession calling for a lengthy study into the various methods of escaping. With the advent of World War II the art of escape became a profession and teams, clubs and even bureaucratic organisations were set up to devote themselves wholly to planning escapes.

This professional approach to the whole subject of escapes has been carried over into peacetime by the highly trained and organised gangs who 'spring' people from prisons as a means of earning a living, not to mention the Secret Services of the world who have decided that they cannot afford to let valuable agents languish in prison.

It may seem that the young man has the edge on the older man when it comes to escaping from a prison. In fact World War II belied this theory. Admittedly in the early stages of that war there were no outside organisations to assist escapes from prison: they came into their own much later in the war. Not surprisingly, therefore, it was the older prisoner with his know-how, patience and experience who tended to be the more successful escaper at this period.

Between 1939 and 1941 the average age of the successful escaper from German prison camps was about thirty-five. Even this average does not give an altogether accurate picture. Some of the most spectacular and difficult escapes were engineered by men who were in their fifties and sixties, such as General Giraud, who had learned how to escape in World War I, and the generals who escaped from Campo Twelve in Italy were all over fifty.

Many of these veterans pointed the way to a professional approach to the whole art of escaping. Today there is an echo of this in the fact that some schools even include courses in the arts of escape in the increasingly popular adventure training schemes which so many of them sponsor.

Fifty years ago it was not an infrequent occurrence for boys, if not girls, to escape from school – sometimes from desperate unhappiness, at others as a result of 'dares'. The usual 'dare' was to get some boy to escape from a dormitory window by means of knotted sheets. Today this is not nearly so prevalent even in boarding schools. What may have seemed a daring feat fifty years ago would seem unremarkable to sophisticated schoolboys of today who have seen the epics of Colditz on film and television screens.

World War II showed that organising escapes was a professional job and that it was unfair and endangering men's lives to leave escaping to the initiative of the individual. When Germany had overrun Europe with her armies in that war the need to rescue key people on the Allied side who had been taken prisoner became of paramount importance. Sections of the Services were set up solely to plan and organise rescue coups, to analyse the mistakes made by failed escapers and to try to profit from their experiences.

In the sphere of espionage today it is very often the planners who are the brave, able men taking the risks and the man about to be rescued or 'sprung' could be a downright coward, frightened of making the effort to escape himself so that he has to be drugged, or made drunk before he can be successfully freed from his imprisonment.

As one who has seen something at first hand of the new technique of escape organised by professionals, especially in the underworld of spies, I think I should add a warning. From time to time there will be somewhat sinister efforts made to urge people to escape against their will. This may seem melodramatic, but it is nonetheless something you may have to guard against.

What is even more confusing is that it takes several forms. A foreign espionage service may wish to encourage the 'escape' of some other young national in order to trap him into their spy network. A nineteen-years-old American boy spending his holiday in the Adriatic fell in love with a Polish girl who had been asked to strike up a friendship with him because it was known that he had studied electronics.

She told him a story about being hounded by the local police. Would he help her to escape over the border? Foolishly he agreed not only to help her, but to escape with her. Only when it was too late did he realise that he had been trapped by a spy ring and that the price for his freedom was certain information on electronic equipment.

It was an awkward predicament. But fortunately X (it would be unfair to name him) did not know as much about electronics as the spy ring expected: all he could tell them was fairly routine stuff which they already knew. In this case ignorance really was bliss, as his captors let him go in disgust.

But not everyone might be as lucky as X.

Escaping won't always be a deliberate matter. Sometimes the man who wishes to escape has no choice. He is put in a situation in which his only hope is survival. Then it is a test of dogged determination and supreme will-power.

In this age of speed and penetration into outer space it is, perhaps, among the airmen of the world in which superhuman urges to escape from odds of ten thousand to one against living. That remarkable writer-airman, Antoine de St Exupéry who disappeared without trace on an air operation in 1944, who was one of the first to use his experience of flying to write splendidly accurate fictional stories about the air, once said of his fellow airmen: 'In the mould of this new profession, a new breed of men has been cast.'

Certainly in the sphere of escaping in the air from crashing planes and similar disasters his words were prophetic. Some of the most amazing escapes of all time have been from the air. If ever you should think that all is lost and death inevitable, it is as well to remember the stories of two airmen, one a Russian, the other a Briton, both of whom survived after escaping from planes without parachutes at great altitudes.

The Russian, Lieutenant, now Lieutenant-Colonel, I M Chisov, fell from an Ilyusihin 4 plane in January, 1942, at a height of 22,000 feet. His plane had been severely damaged, he had no parachute and he crashed at an acute angle on a snow-covered, steep slope, sliding to the bottom. The angle at which he landed and the softness of the snow may have

Escape in the Air: Sergeant Ward smothers the flames on Wellington bomber on 7 July 1941

contributed to saving his life, though he received some spinal injuries and a fractured pelvis.

Flight-Sergeant Nicholas Alkemade, aged twenty-one, did not quite reach this record. He was a member of a crew of a Royal Air Force Lancaster bomber which was hit at a height of 18,000 feet in March, 1944. His aircraft received a direct hit and was enveloped in flames within a few seconds. Nicholas, too, jumped out without a parachute: there was neither time, nor opportunity for any other action. Down he went towards German soil and, though his record in terms of height was not as great as that of the Russian, in terms of achievement it was even more remarkable. For Nicholas's fall was broken by the soft upper branches of a tall fir tree. No doubt these acted as a kind of buffer to ease the last few yards of his descent. At any rate he landed in a deep drift of soft snow and survived without a single broken bone or other damage.

Escape in the Air, 1918

THE PILOT STANDING ON A WING, KEEPING CONTROL, AND SIDE-SLIPPING HIS MACHINE DOWN SO THAT THE FLAMES ARE BLOWN AWAY FROM HIM AND HIS OBSERVER: THE OBSERVER FIRING AT THE ENEMY—BEFORE THE "CRASH."

Britain's last Lancaster bomber

Thus escape in such circumstances often depends upon the tenacity by which a man hangs on to life as long as is humanly possible, often long after others would give up all hope.

There is the story of the longest recorded survival alone on a raft on the open ocean. Second Steward Poon Lim, of Hongkong, of the British Merchant Navy, was serving aboard the ss Ben Lomond when it was torpedoed in the Atlantic Ocean 750 miles off the Azores at 11.45 am on 23 November, 1942. He spent 133 days alone on a raft until he was picked up by a Brazilian fishing vessel off Salinas, Brazil, on 5 April, 1943, and was able at last to walk ashore.

For this feat Poon Lim was awarded the British Empire Medal in July, 1943. It was a tribute to his courage, will-power and ability to fight for survival with assistance from no other human being.

Poon Lim was twenty-five years old when he underwent his

ordeal. As a youth he had been keen on basketball and football and had spent much of his childhood fishing 'which was to stand me in very good stead later on'.

Most of his shipmates perished when the ship was torpedoed. Poon Lim managed to reach a raft that was floating on the water after his ship had sunk. There was nobody else on that raft.

'It was about six feet square and of standard design, with containers fore and aft,' said Poon Lim in telling his story afterwards. 'One contained water and in the other were provisions including chocolate, barley sugar, biscuits, fish paste and a bottle of lime juice. There was also Verey light apparatus, some "yellow smoke" for signalling.

'My first meal was of barley sugar. My shoes and trousers had been washed away while I was in the water and my vest and pants were covered in oil. So I took them off, washed them in the sea and hung them out to dry, and, as night came on, I fell asleep.

'I awoke cold and shivering, naked in the rain. My pants had been washed away and my vest was soaking. However, the sun came out later and I got warm and dry again. I took careful stock of my provisions and decided to eat six biscuits a day, or two per meal.'

MR. POON LIM.

Poon Lim, the Chinese steward who spent 133 days alone on a raft after his ship had been torpedoed in the Atlantic, is in England as a guest of the Government. He has been awarded the B.E.M. He was the sole survivor of fifty-five in a freighter, but he has refused to discuss his experiences, thinking it discourtesy before he has told the King about them.

Poon Lim's first problem was how to fish. The only rope aboard the raft was too thick so he had to unravel it and spin a line for himself. He made a hook out of the fastener of the yellow smoke container. For bait he made a paste out of biscuit powder, but found this washed off too quickly. Eventually he found some barnacles on the side of the raft and with their meat he baited his hook.

'My first catch was a brownish-coloured fish with hard scales. "Little fish, you have saved my life!" I said as I cut it up. My second catch was much better – a small shark of about ten pounds.

'This I also cut up for bait, but the fish would not take its meat. I noticed, however, that the blood and part of the entrails of the shark attracted a school of whiting. I tried tying pieces of the entrails on to the line without using the hook. In this way I scooped several of the small fish on to the

Provisions for 133 days on a raft

deck and felt very pleased with myself. In my home village the housewives dry their clothes on a *loo-tai*, a kind of platform on top of the house. I rigged my lines on the four posts of the raft in imitation of a *loo-tai* and dried my fish in this way.'

After seven days Poon Lim sighted a steamer and he fired all the Verey lights and used up the yellow smoke, but, close as the ship appeared to be, she steamed on without altering course. This was Poon Lim's darkest moment of all.

'However, I cheered myself by singing songs from Chinese operas and my success with fishing made me feel better. To replenish my supplies of water there was plenty of rain at times, but there were also drought periods that caused me concern until I learned to condense water from the humid atmosphere by dangling my water can in the sea.

'On the hundredth day, as near as I can guess, I struck a

bad patch. The fish would not take for some reason and I had eaten all my provisions, dried fish and bait included. For five days I was without food.

'On the fifth day some small birds settled on the raft. They were black with white spots on their foreheads. I waited till nightfall and then when they were asleep, I seized one and tied it up. Altogether I caught thirteen of these birds, but one got away. They tasted like the fish.

'I used parts of the birds for bait and caught more fish. I spent all my time improving my fishing lines and trying new ways of fishing. I found that by swishing my bait through the water and dibbling it up and down, I could catch more fish. This discovery probably saved my life.

'I was so hungry that I ate some of the fish raw.'

As Poon Lim approached the Brazilian coast he noticed that the water was changing colour and that there were some fish like salmon which suggested he was near a river mouth, in fact, he was at the approaches to the Amazon.

Even then Poon Lim had some more bad luck. He spotted a fishing vessel, but failed to attract its attention; he saw other ships which only disappeared over the horizon. Then an aeroplane flew over him and dropped a flare. A few days later a Brazilian fishing craft rescued him.

Although he was able to walk ashore, Poon Lim went to hospital for 45 days. 'I was a bit thin when I landed, but I never had a headache the whole time I was on the raft and I had slept soundly every night. I do not attribute my survival to any philosophy peculiar to China unless it is that we Chinese are very practical. I concentrated all my thoughts and efforts on getting food and water.'

Later Poon Lim was able to tell the full story of his 133-day ordeal to King George VI.

Poon Lim is the supreme example of the lone escaper on the open seas. One might think it would be easier when there are two or three on a raft, that each has something to contribute towards survival. History suggests it does not work out that way.

There have been a number of examples of whole families in small craft who have been lost at sea with inadequate provisions and have had to use all their ingenuity to survive. In nearly all cases there have been quarrels, violent disagreements and possibly more obstacles to survival than in the case of the loner.

One has to remember that any fight for survival is a test of character. It may sound shocking, but sometimes the strongest character is the most unpleasant and yet he is the only person who enables some, if not all, to survive. It does not mean that he thinks solely of himself.

There is the classic case of the yawl *Mignonette* which capsized in the South Atlantic in 1884. The captain, Thomas Dudley, and a crew of three, including a cabin-boy, were cast adrift in a dinghy without food or water, the situation made worse by the fact that the cabin-boy had dropped the one and only container of fresh water into the sea.

The yawl was being sailed out to Australia for her new owner. On the voyage out the boat stopped at Madeira and it was here that Thomas Dudley rescued a Portuguese girl from drowning. It was touch and go and even when the others had given up hope, Dudley bent over the inanimate figure and pressed his lips against hers, tugging at her lungs to breathe life into her.

It transpired that the girl was an orphan who wanted to end her life. The Portuguese all thought she was mad, but Dudley, a compassionate, God-fearing man, gave her an address in Australia through which she could always reach him, if she needed help.

Thus a life was saved in Madeira at the risk of his own life, while the very same man proposed in mid-Atlantic to do away with the life of the cabin-boy. Thomas Dudley was married, a devoted husband and father, even a regular Church-goer, yet when they had been at sea several days with only two tins of turnips for provisions for four men, he cold-bloodedly proposed killing the cabin-boy for the rest of them to survive.

Horrible it may sound and yet, if one is to understand how people have escaped from seemingly impossible situations the case of the killing of this cabin-boy needs to be understood. Dudley, Stephens and Brooks (the other two crew members) and the cabin-boy, Richard Parker, were at the mercy of the scorching sun and freezing nights for more than three weeks with virtually no food and for water only what they could catch in an oilskin when it rained.

As the Mignonette went down: Sketch by Edwin Stephens, the mate

Dudley, who had been described by his previous employers as a man 'of excellent character, able to tackle any job requiring seamanship, courageous and with real power of command', put to Stephens and Brooks the brutal truth: Richard Parker was useless in their battle for survival, he was not merely sick, but obviously dying and in the direst misery. Their only hope of food was to kill him and eat his flesh.

Curiously Dudley had read a book by Edgar Allan Poe on the voyage, entitled 'The Narrative of Arthur Gordon Pym', a story in which castaways in a boat drew lots to determine who should be sacrificed to become food for the rest, the victim so selected being named Richard Parker, by an extraordinary coincidence the actual name of the *Mignonette's* cabin-boy.

Dudley, the captain, was prepared to draw lots and risk sacrificing himself to save his starving companions. The others would not agree. Perhaps Dudley saw the force of their arguments. He realised Parker was dying and that there was little chance of saving his life.

Of the other two crew members one had lost his nerve, the other had no fire in his belly. Dudley knew that if three of them were to survive, it could only be through his taking charge of the situation.

He put the case to the other two. Between them, if they died, two women and eight children would suffer. He pointed out that the cabin-boy was dying, that he was unmarried and

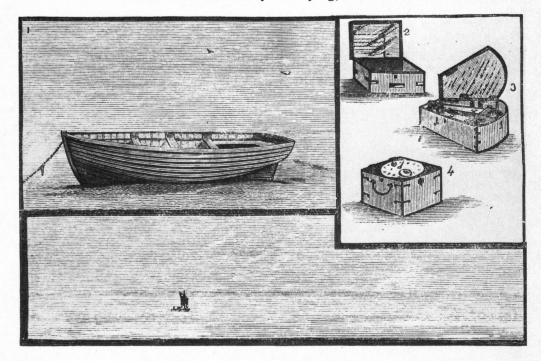

Sketches drawn by Edwin Stephens, the mate

had no dependants. But nobody wanted to plunge in the knife that would end his life.

Finally Dudley put this proposal: 'If there is no vessel in sight and no rain by sunrise tomorrow, I think we had better kill the lad. Do you agree?'

Silently he got assent.

Their nineteenth day afloat dawned with the same bleak horizon, without a single craft in sight. There was no hint of rain to come, to provide the much-needed water. It was then that Dudley took charge and, after offering up a prayer for young Parker, slit his throat with a pen-knife.

Dudley never denied that he was the ringleader in this killing. In his statement which was given in court when back in England he was eventually tried for the killing of Parker, he said 'We caught the blood in the baler and drank it while it was warm. Then we stripped the body, cut it open and took out his liver and heart and we ate the liver while it was warm.'

Then on 28 July, 1884, the survivors were picked up by the German barque, *Montezuma*, whose captain ordered the dinghy to be hauled aboard. It was quickly realised that the cabin-boy was not merely dead, but that he had been at least partially eaten. They called for a doctor's report before making arrangements to commit his body to the sea.

'They all told the same story, calmly and without

hesitation,' said the German captain, 'and they expressed horror and remorse for what they had done. But I don't think it dawned on them that they had committed a murder and would be liable to be tried for that crime. I warned them that I should have to inform the authorities at a British port of what had occurred, and they understood this. But the implications of my warning were lost on them. They were quite apathetic.'

When they were landed at Falmouth the men were charged with the murder of the cabin-boy. In due course the death sentence was passed on them. But, such was the tradition of life afloat in those days, that among many seamen it was almost an unwritten law that cannibalism was permissible in certain circumstances. Eventually the death sentence was commuted to six months' imprisonment without hard labour.

Dudley himself emigrated to Australia with his family to seek a new life where nobody would know about his past. But one echo from his past did reappear. The girl he had saved from drowning in Madeira turned up in Australia to greet him. For Dudley, who had risked everything to ensure his family's future, this posed serious problems.

Late in life he was confronted by the romantic devotion of the girl whose life he had saved, one who counted on him to give her a reason for staying alive.

For Tom Dudley himself retribution ultimately came in the most horrible form. He was the first man in Australia to die from bubonic plague.

Chapter 2

Escapes which have changed the course of history

As we have already seen, the successful escaper can be a scoundrel, a murderer, a hero or just a tremendously level-headed, practical young man like Poon Lim. Or he may be someone with a burning desire to see justice done, like Alfred Hinds.

Generally speaking, whatever category he comes into, he is a remarkable man in some way or other. So it is not surprising that some escapes have changed the course of history.

There have been so many of these that it is difficult to know where to begin. But perhaps the first and most remarkable of escapes to change the course of history was the escape of the Holy Family from King Herod.

The King's 'Wise Men' had spotted a bright new star in the west, one which could quite easily be seen in King Herod's chamber. They reported to the King that this meant that 'a princely babe was born that night, No king could e'er destroy'.

It was a rash statement even for 'Wise Men' to make to an overbearing King. Herod's reaction was predictable. He was furious. One version of what happened, as it comes down to us by legend, is that Herod said if the Wise Men's claim was true, 'this roasted cock that lies in the dish shall crow three times'. And the story goes that the cock did indeed crow three times in the dish in which it lay.

But whatever happened to that cock, or if this is merely an embellishment of the legend, the truth is that King Herod immediately ordered that all children under two years of age should promptly be slain and that the 'Holy Child' must be found.

Warned in a dream of the possible fate that awaited them if they remained in Bethlehem, Joseph, Mary and the baby Jesus fled by night and crossed into Egypt, remaining there until Herod was dead.

The flight into Egypt

Yet another prophet, Mohammed of Mecca, would not have brought his philosophy and religion to the world without a well-planned escape. At an early age he had original ideas about how people should live and conduct themselves and he made a number of converts to his way of thinking.

But there was considerable opposition to Mohammed's teaching. He was forced to advise his followers to move to Medina in small groups so that they should not attract too much attention and it is from this time – the date of the flight – from which Mohammedans today date their calendar, in the year 622.

Mohammed waited until all the groups had safely left for Medina before following on himself. He was determined to safeguard his followers first.

At last Mohammed received warning that his enemies had plotted to kill him. Pretending to go to bed, he slipped his mantle over a sleeping servant and disappeared through a window in disguise. For the next few days Mohammed and his loyal ally, Abu Bekr, hid in a cave in the vicinity while the killers searched everywhere for him.

Then, when the quest died down, they made the journey to Medina by camel. He was cautious up to the last moment. He had not seen his followers for many months and he could not be sure whether they had remained loyal to him. He sent a message into the city, asking for certain people to come out and greet him.

He need not have worried. Many tribes came out to welcome him to Medina, crying: 'Greetings, O Prophet! Stay with us, we have all the means of defending you.'

Perhaps no escape helped to change the course of history more than Winston Churchill's escape from the Boers in the South African War. True, the changes that came about occurred forty years later when Churchill, by becoming British Prime Minister, saved Britain from total collapse against Germany.

In 1899 Churchill, then twenty-five years old, was a war correspondent for the *Morning Post,* covering the Boer War, in which the crack troops of Britain had taken a severe mauling from the clever guerrilla tactics and raids of the Boer farmer commandoes.

In mid-November that year Churchill accompanied a Captain Haldane on a reconnaissance expedition deep into Boer territory. There were some 120 men in an armoured train, comprising five wagons, an engine in the middle of them and a somewhat outdated seven-pounder muzzle-loading gun.

The purpose of the expedition may have been laudable, but the means of carrying it out was hardly effective. The ancient train belched forth clouds of steam and smoke and, in the silent countryside could hardly fail to draw the attention of the Boer scouts who were placed on horses at key points.

Winston Churchill

The Boers halted the train, placing a rock on the track, and while the soldiers worked hard to clear the track and get moving again, they came under heavy fire. The engine, crammed with wounded, eventually got away. Churchill was taken prisoner and imprisoned in the States Model Schools.

Long afterwards Churchill wrote: 'When my armoured train was thrown off the rails by the Boers in the South African War and I had to try to clear the line under fire, I was obliged to keep getting in and out of the cab of the engine . . . I therefore took off my Mauser pistol, which got in the way. But for this I should, forty minutes later, have fired two or three shots at twenty yards at a mounted burgher named Botha, who summoned me to surrender. If I had killed him on that day, the history of South Africa would certainly have been different, and almost certainly less fortunate. This was the Botha who afterwards became Commander-in-Chief of

the Boers and later the Prime Minister of the South African Union.

'But for his authority and vigour the South African rebellion which broke out at the beginning of the Great War (World War I) might never have been nipped "in the bud".'

It was from Lourenco Marques in Portuguese territory in South Africa that Churchill sent to the *Morning Post* on 22 December, 1899, the story of his escape from the Boers. It created a great sensation at the time because the Boers regarded Churchill as even more dangerous as a war correspondent than he might have been as a soldier. Notices were placed everywhere offering a reward for him alive or dead.

Yet, typically Churchillian, he stated that 'before I had been an hour in captivity I resolved to escape'. For a whole month he thought of nothing else, turning over various plans in his mind, but rejecting most of them.

The States Model Schools, where he was held in custody, were surrounded on two sides by an iron grille and on the other two by a corrugated iron fence about ten feet high. Churchill knew these were not insuperable barriers to an active, healthy young man, but they were guarded on the inside by sentries fifty yards apart, armed with rifles and revolvers.

It was therefore a question of watching the movements of the sentries and trying to detect a weakness in their precautions. It meant pacing the quadrangle and calculating the one moment when detection of an escape attempt was most difficult. Churchill noted that the electric lights in the middle of the quadrangle were powerful and illuminating, but that by some mischance cut off the sentries beyond them from looking at the eastern wall.

As the young escape planner worked it out: 'From behind

The States Model School, Pretoria, drawn by Churchill himself

the lights all seemed darkness by contrast. The first thing was therefore to pass the two sentries near the offices. It was necessary to hit the exact moment when both their backs should be turned together. After the wall was scaled, we should be in the garden of the villa next door.'

Even if this plan succeeded, it was impossible to tell what would happen once Churchill got over the wall. But it was the one hope of escape. At the same time it was a gamble with death, for if the plan went wrong a sentry could hit his target at fifteen yards.

On 11 December Churchill decided to make the escape. It is interesting that this bold, brave character expressed in his despatch all the fears that go through the minds of most escapers. He tried to read a book, but gave it up. He played chess – so badly that he lost. But, alas, on this day after a wait of two hours the escape plan was ruined because one of the sentries stood exactly opposite the part of the wall where the attempt was to be made.

But the next day, when desperation called for risks, Churchill strolled the quadrangle to sum up the position. He watched the sentries; then he saw one of them walk up to a colleague and engage him in conversation. Their backs were turned.

This was the moment he had been waiting for. Churchill ran to the wall, climbed it swiftly, lay flat on the top for a moment to observe the sentries (they were still chatting), and then dropped quietly down into the garden fifteen yards away.

Nearby was a house and from here a man appeared, walking in Churchill's direction until he stopped ten yards away. Had he been spotted? What should he do? Should he remain silent and still and hope he would not be seen, or should he pose as a Boer detective on the look-out for an escaped prisoner. Churchill wisely settled for remaining still in the dark background. Eventually the man went away with another who had joined him.

Boldly, during the night, Churchill, humming a tune for the sheer exhilaration of escape, made his way into Pretoria. He was bang inside the enemy's country and he knew nobody to whom he could apply for help. He realised that he had to move fast; that his escape would be known by dawn and that a hue and cry with a reward for his capture alive or dead would be issued immediately.

His main disability was that he could not speak a word of Dutch or Kaffir, which meant that it would be almost impossible for him to get either food or directions.

He hit upon a simple plan: to follow the track of the Delgoa Bay Railway. But first he had to find the railroad.

Here was the improvising genius of the Churchill mind at its best. He found the line, but realised that he could not just walk 300 miles to the frontier. He needed to sneak aboard a

£25.—.—

(vijf en twintig pond stg.)
belooning uitgeloofd door
de Sub-Commissie van Wijk V
voor den Specialen Constabel
dezer wijk, die den ontvluchte
krijgsgevangene
      Churchill
levend of dood te dezer kantore
aflevert.—

Namens de Sub-Comm.
Wijk V
Lodk. de Haas
Sec.

Translation.

£25

(Twenty-five Pounds stg.) REWARD is offered by the Sub-Commission of the fifth division, on behalf of the Special Constable of the said division, to anyone who brings the escaped prisioner of war

CHURCHILL,

dead or alive to this office.

For the Sub-Commission of the fifth division,
(Signed) LODK. de HAAS, Sec.

NOTE.—The Original Reward for the arrest of Winston Churchill on his escape from Pretoria, posted on the Government House of Pretoria, brought to England by the Hon. Henry Massham, and is now the property of W. R. Barton.

train and hide anywhere on it, under the seats, on the roof, on the couplings. All he had to sustain him was four chocolate bars, as his friend who was to have escaped with him and failed to make it had all the vital equipment of escape such as compasses, meat lozenges and a map.

But he set out walking along the line at a fast rate, sometimes having to make detours to avoid the pickets who guarded the bridges. All he hoped was that sooner or later a train would appear and he would be able to get aboard. At last his luck was in. A train slowed down into a station and, as it left, gathering speed slowly, Churchill hurled himself on the trucks, 'clutched at something, missed, clutched again, missed again, grasped some sort of hand-hold, was swung off my feet — my toes bumping on the line, and with a struggle seated myself on the couplings of the fifth truck down the front of the train. It was a goods train and the trucks were full of sacks, soft sacks covered with coal dust. I crawled on top and burrowed in among them'.

For hours he slept and he awoke with a dreadful thirst. His first thought was that he must leave the train to try to get a drink. Then perhaps he could join another train that night.

He hurled himself off the train and landed awkwardly but not too badly injured in a ditch. Luckily he was able to find a clear pool where he could quench his thirst. But to find another train was not easy. He had to continue to walk along the line to avoid the sentinels on the bridges and hope that eventually he would get a train running to Lourenco Marques.

Meanwhile the hunt for Winston Churchill had been stepped up. The Boers regarded him as an enemy worth recapturing at all costs: his escapades as a Hussar in the Sudan and India were well known in South Africa and the politically-minded Boers were well aware that he was not only

Churchill, waiting for the night to come, from a sketch by himself

'I hurled myself on the trucks . . .'

a kinsman of the Duke of Marlborough, but the son of Lord Randolph Churchill. Telegrams of his description were sent out all over the country, 3,000 photographs of Churchill were printed and every train was ordered to be searched.

At last the train young Churchill had been waiting for came along. It was scheduled for Lourenco Marques and standing in a siding. This time Churchill was determined not to have to leave a train to quench his thirst: he filled a bottle of water to drink on the way. In stifling heat, among sacks, he expected the journey might last thirty-six hours, which was bad enough under such conditions; instead, it took sixty hours.

The main fear was that of the train being searched, which made sleep a risky operation. Once they did search the very truck he was in, but did not delve deep enough to find him.

At last Churchill reached Delgoa Bay and safety and, in a filthy condition, he scrambled out of the train to freedom, then to file his despatch to his newspaper and to add the words 'the reader who may persevere through this hurried account will understand why I write them with a feeling of triumph, and better than triumph, a feeling of pure joy'.

Of all nationalities perhaps the French have the greatest talents for the art of escaping. It may be their logical minds, allied to their undoubtedly imaginative genius, but, throughout history, including even the great Napoleon himself, they have revealed a positive genius, almost, one might say, a vocation for escape.

In modern times two Frenchmen who escaped against great odds not only deserve a niche in the archives of great escapists, but a brief note or two on how they helped to change the course of history. Curiously enough, they were totally dissimilar and, though both devoted to defeating the

Germans, each had something to contribute to the forging of post-war Europe, even if politically they were opposite sides of the fence.

The elder of these was General Henri Giraud, who set up something of a record by escaping in World War I and World War II. However, it was his second escape, in 1942, which was the most momentous and one which did a great deal to boost French morale at a time when it was at a low ebb.

Giraud left St Cyr, the French military academy, as one of the most brilliant cadets it had ever produced. But he was dogged by bad luck in war time. In World War I, when a captain, he was wounded in a bayonet charge leading a Zouave detachment at Charleroi, and left behind on the field. Even his comrades were convinced he was dead. The Germans took him to a prison camp in Belgium, but no special precautions were taken as they believed him to be dangerously ill and quite incapable of escaping.

They reckoned without knowing the determination of Henri Honoré Giraud. Before his wounds had healed he not only escaped from the prison camp, but showed his lively initiative by pretending to be a Belgian and joining a circus as a performer. Eventually when he got to Brussels he was helped to escape into Holland by Nurse Edith Cavell, who had devoted herself to assisting Allied officers to escape.

Giraud made his way from Holland to Britain and eventually rejoined his regiment in France. Between the wars he served in Africa, taught at the *Ecole de Guerra* in Paris and, when the Second World War came, was appointed commander-in-chief of the Allied Forces in Laon.

Giraud was faced with the full thrust of the German break-through in the Ardennes. He was then sixty-one years old, but this did not deter him from going up to the front to see whether the German advance could be checked. Inevitably he

General Henri Giraud with President Roosevelt

MISS EDITH CAVELL
DIED FOR HER COUNTRY OCT. 12th 1915.

was captured by the Germans who, realising his reputation as a general, were anxious to appear magnanimous to him. Would he give his word as an officer and a gentleman that he would not try to escape? It was quite clear that the Germans hoped to use Giraud as a puppet to exploit in propaganda against the Allies.

Giraud resolutely declined to give any such undertaking. Furious, the Germans dispatched him to the fortress of Königstein, an impregnable prison situated on a cliff 150 feet high, specially designed to cope with important prisoners. This time the Germans were determined that Giraud should not escape.

They were wrong. Not even his age deterred the gallant general from immediately planning a getaway. Indeed his age plus his experience helped him to plan rather better than in World War I. First he determined to improve his

General Giraud, shortly after his capture in May 1940

knowledge of German. He could speak it a little, but he continued to speak it daily until he could manage it without a suspicion of a French accent. He tried it out on his guards and asked them how it sounded; he listened to their criticisms and then practised it alone in the silence of his cell.

Giraud knew that unless he could speak German like a native he would never be able to escape from Königstein for long. He managed to borrow a map of the neighbouring countryside and he copied this out, then memorised it before finally burning it.

Fortunately there were others inside France who were anxious to assist Giraud's escape. Without their assistance it is doubtful if he could ever have got away from Königstein, one of the most impregnable of prisons.

Friends sent him packages tied with twine and he used this to make himself a rope. When he had completed it, however, his experience told him that it would not be strong enough to support him.

Through an invalided prisoner who had been repatriated he sent a code to his wife. He was allowed to write letters home, and, using this code in what seemed to be perfectly ordinary letters, he indicated that his basic requirement was copper wire to strengthen his rope. Letter by letter he gave his ideas on how he could escape and what could be done to help him.

His wife passed the coded letters on to his main helpers. They sent him a ham in which was hidden copper wire. Luckily for Giraud the ham got through the censors and he was able to complete his plans.

All this scheming had taken the best part of two years. He now had the means to escape – a rope, strengthened by copper wire, which would bear his weight – but the problem was how to get away in the blue uniform of a French general. His raincoat would pass for civilian clothing, but what he badly needed was an ordinary hat. This, too, as a result of coded messages, duly arrived. It was a Tyrolean hat and once again it was hidden inside a ham.

Perhaps the Germans had been too careless with General Giraud. On the other hand maybe they thought that, as long as they were winning the war, he might be won over to their side. It was on 17 April, 1942, that they learned the error of their ways. On that morning Giraud went out on to the balcony overlooking the sentry walk.

He had tied tightly together a package containing his raincoat, the Tyrolean hat, some chocolates and biscuits, and fixed this to his waist. For days previously he had counted the seconds while the sentry below passed backwards and forwards; it was now only a matter of calculating the right moment for him to make his getaway.

His laboriously-made rope of twine, reinforced with copper wire, was all ready to be thrown over the wall the

Königstein Fortress

moment the sentry was furthest from him. Giraud swifty knotted the top of the rope to the balcony and began his 150-foot drop to the ground. Wisely he had provided himself with gloves, but even so the descent was painful and cut his skin.

Giraud's escape was one against all physical odds. He was in his sixties, his wounds from World War II still gave him pain and, in the descent from Königstein Prison, they caused him great agony. By the time he reached the ground he could only limp slowly away from the jail.

He reached a small wood, shaved off his moustache, put on his Tyrolean hat and raincoat and, despite the acute pain caused by his wounds, managed to limp to a bridge at Schandau, some five miles away.

Alone and unaided, Giraud could have achieved little. But the coded messages had worked well; friends not only in France, but agents outside that country had been prepared to assist him. He was met at the bridge by a man who took him to a nearby station. There the man gave him a suitcase containing some clothes, forged identity papers and money.

Changing in the lavatory on the train, Giraud was able to adopt his new identity before the alarm for his arrest had been circulated. But he did not have long to wait. A full description of him was wired around Germany within hours. And that full description mentioned that Giraud was over six feet in height, something he could not disguise.

But the general had not wasted his two years of escape planning: he had long ago realised that the search for so important a prisoner as himself would be as thorough as the Germans could make it. Instructions would go out to the Gestapo as well as the Army police to catch Giraud at all costs. His tactics were to travel by train, but to change trains frequently, edging nearer the French border all the time, but never staying too long in one train.

On three occasions Giraud was actually leaving a train as Gestapo officers were boarding it; on another occasion when the Gestapo actually searched a train he was on, he saved himself by entering into conversation on the war with a German officer in the *Afrika Korps* seated beside him. On another occasion he feigned fatigue and actually asked a Gestapo man to help him on to the train.

The quest for Giraud was so intense that it was impossible for him to cross the border into France. German guards were posted at all frontier posts on the railway: they had strict instructions to stop all men of six feet in height. So the general detoured back into Germany and headed for the Swiss frontier. It was finally through Switzerland that he made his escape. The Germans insisted that the Swiss should send him back; the Swiss, arguing that they were neutrals in the war, refused. On the other hand the Swiss would not let him go into France.

The Gestapo still hunted him in Switzerland: their agents closed in on his hiding place. But Giraud this time changed cars every few miles. Eventually he got back to France.

But he was still forced to go into hiding. The Germans demanded his return and, though Marshal Pétain refused to send him back, a Nazi plot to assassinate the general meant he had to disappear again.

When General Giraud eventually emerged it was at one of the most crucial moments of the war. By this time the Americans and British were planning the invasion of North Africa. They agreed that Giraud would make an admirable leader of a pro-Allied French force. A signal was sent to France that Giraud must be smuggled out to Algeria.

A few nights later a British submarine was sent to France to pick up Giraud and bring him to North Africa where he helped to pave the way for a victory over the Germans.

While General Giraud was swiftly removed from the sphere of political influence by General De Gaulle, another and younger Frenchman was also planning to escape from prison. This young man was Pierre Mendès-France, perhaps the only Prime Minister of any country who actually bombed his own capital.

Mendès-France, who had held office in the French Government at the age of thirty-one, had quit politics and joined the French Air Force when he saw how France was being undermined by defeatism in the face of German threats. After the fall of France to the Nazi armies he went over to North Africa, hoping to carry on the fight from there.

He was, however, arrested on the orders of the Vichy Government and sentenced to six years' imprisonment, loss of rank and deprived of all civil rights. Bitterly he told the French judge who tried him: 'I hope you will recover your

Pierre Mendès–France

On one occasion the Gestapo actually helped Giraud off a train

Mendès-France in front of the military tribunal of Clermont-Ferrand

sense of honour one day. You work well for Hitler and your personal advancement.'

Yet it was not until a month before he became Prime Minister of France in 1954 that the judgement of the Vichy Government tribunal was reversed and the conviction wiped out for ever.

From the moment he went to prison, Mendès-France started to plot his escape. Again, like Giraud, he planned methodically and logically. He knew that to escape he must be absolutely fit. He decided that his first objective must be not merely to get fit, but to tone up his muscles. Not only was he unused to athletics or violent exercise, but he was almost drained of strength through months of illness.

He exercised surreptitiously, methodically practising breathing exercises, learning to take deep breaths, draw in his shoulder-blades until they were taut, then to hold his breath while he lifted the heaviest weight he could find.

Years later he pooh-poohed the merits of his planned escape: 'I had had no apprenticeship for this sort of task. I hadn't been a burglar or a housebreaker. I had to depend on what I had read in fiction. All the best escapes – certainly the perfect ones – are those you read in detective novels. I just had to have the file, the knotted sheets and all that goes with a classical escape in the best detective story traditions.'

His first plan was to save money to keep him going while he escaped. As a prisoner he had a certain amount of pocket-money. This he saved until he had accumulated 5,000 franc notes, a substantial amount in those days. He tucked this money away in the lining of his cap.

There were also occasional opportunities for making money by the sale and barter of foodstuffs and cigarettes. This aroused no suspicion because, as Mendès himself smilingly admitted afterwards: 'They attributed my trafficking to my Jewish ancestry.'

In the prison workshop he found a rubber stamp and used this for forging himself a set of papers. For a promise to supply another prisoner with five packets of cigarettes a week he obtained ration-cards and the all-important permanent ration-card which would enable him to get renewals when the other cards were out of date. He also got some identity papers.

These items cost him dearly in food. Quite a lot of his daily bread ration disappeared this way. The forging of the identity papers and ration-cards proved a tedious and difficult task for a man who was an amateur in the art of forgery. The rubber stamp was useful, but the chief problem was the erasing of details on the papers before he could complete the work.

Normal methods of erasure would have been easily detected. Then he remembered – probably from his student days when he studied a little chemistry – that permanganate could be a satisfactory eraser. But how to get permanganate? He recalled that permanganate of potash was used as a gargle for sore throats. He used this excuse to get some from the prison hospital.

Food parcels were allowed into prison and from these Mendès-France ate only perishable foods. He hoarded such items as sugar, tins of sardines and bars of chocolate: these were to provide him with vital rations while he was making his escape.

It was not easy to hide such hoardings as his cell was frequently searched. But when his cell was scrutinised he paid particular attention to the places that were overlooked by the warder. He noticed that in winter nobody ever bothered to search in the cinders in the stove. So the cinders became a favourite hiding-place, thereby depriving him of regular fires. But even this he turned to his advantage by selling his meagre coal ration to make more money. In the summer he stuffed his hoard into the stove-pipes and sewed some of the smaller articles into his clothes.

He acquired a rusty hacksaw which he found lying about in the prison yard, and rumour has it that this was the instrument with which he finally broke out of prison. However, Mendès' own version is that the vital weapon in his escape was a file sent in to him by a friend. But this was after he discovered that so many of the hacksaw's teeth were damaged that it was useless for cutting through the bars of his cell window.

He realised that he needed a disguise, so he let his beard grow. He also acquired a pipe and a pair of spectacles – the former to give an excuse for putting his hand up to his face to keep it partly hidden and the latter to put on as soon as he left prison.

Moved to the prison hospital, he was shown to a room occupied by other prisoners. This he knew would be fatal to

His forged identity card

his plans, so he made a fuss and demanded that, as an officer, he was entitled to a cell to himself.

'You have been sentenced for desertion, so you are no longer an officer,' he was informed.

'But,' argued Mendès, 'I have appealed against my sentence, and until my appeal is heard I am still an officer.'

The other inmates of the room regarded this argument as a display of arrogance directed against them. But finally it was agreed that Mendès should be given a cell to himself.

This was the chance he had waited for. As long as he was in the hospital block of the prison his chances of escape were favourable. It was a race against time. The bars of the cell window must be sawn through without delay while he was alone.

But when Mendès tried his file on the bars, he felt the cold sweat of terror. The bars were not of cast iron, but of steel. On cast iron a file bites smoothly and silently: on steel it hisses and screams.

'I realised that unless I thought out some method of overcoming this problem, I should be detected in no time at all,' he said afterwards. 'My cell was next to a room where the prison staff slept. You see, they were taking no chances with me when I asked for a private cell.'

Yet Mendès-France managed to solve this problem by what he called somewhat sarcastically 'a musical synchronisation'. He noted that the prison staff snored at regular intervals. He timed the intervals and periods taken up by snoring. Then he calculated that 'snoring time' would give him a chance to saw through the bars by morning. He even noted the nights of the week when the snoring periods reached their peak. Doubtless these coincided with the nights on which alcoholic consumption was highest. No detail was overlooked. It was all as mathematical as a game of chess. The man of figures was proving a match for the ablest of housebreakers.

When the snores rose to a crescendo he went to work with his file, sawing fast and sweating profusely. When the snores stopped, he ceased work. Indeed, he did not dare wait until they stopped: he slowed down the moment the snores became quieter.

Meanwhile he had studied carefully the whole layout of the prison outside his cell window. He knew exactly what he had to do, how he had to measure his jumps. His chief worry was that the cuts in the bars of the window would be noticed by a warder. How could he cover them up? He remembered that he had acquired some eye-black for use as a disguise and by mixing this with cinder dust and smearing it on the bars he was able to cover up the tell-tale cuts.

Then came what could have been a fatal blow to all his carefully laid plans. On 20 June, 1941, his lawyer came to tell him that his appeal against sentence had been dismissed. The prison authorities promptly put another man in his cell.

'I suppose the conversation
only lasted a few minutes'

Should he take his fellow-prisoner into his confidence? Mendès decided against this partly on the grounds that he knew nothing about the man, but equally because he did not wish to involve him unfairly. But while he was pondering on what best to do, the fellow-prisoner, Douhet, unsuspectingly offered the solution. He complained that he had not been feeling well and was sleeping badly. Could Mendès give him a couple of asprins? Mendès did better than that: he gave him four and assured him he would sleep all the sounder.

It seemed like hours before Douhet dozed off. But finally Mendès was able to make his getaway. A few deft touches with the file and he was able to open the bars of the window. He put out the sheets and secured one end to the stumps of the bars. It was a dark night; lowering his suitcase, which was wrapped up in a coat, he squeezed himself through the window and began his descent.

'I slid down easily enough, crossed the courtyard and reached the foot of the wall opposite. I had twenty-four feet to climb. I knew even in the dark which stone to grip, where to put my hands and feet. There wasn't a cranny I wasn't sure of.'

He wasn't boasting intentionally. To him this was just a recital of the facts. For a man with so precise a mind as Mendès-France it would have seemed incredibly stupid if he had not anticipated such details.

'In a few seconds I reached the top of the wall and wriggled down until I was lying flat. Dark as it was, a silhouette might have been seen.'

What happened then was a crisis that was lightened by a certain amount of, if not actual fun, at least an appeal to Mendès-France's sense of humour.

In his autobiographical *Liberté, Liberté, Chérie*, Mendès-France has given his own account of what then happened.

A big tree stood immediately in front of the wall where he lay. Under its branches two young lovers were discussing plans for their future. The boy had a proposition to make. The girl was doubtful about it. Minutes passed while the love-talk continued. Mendès waited, silent, but impatient. He knew that soon the local cinema would finish its show and the streets would be full of people.

'I suppose the conversation only lasted a few minutes, but to me it seemed like a century. The boy knew just what he wanted. The girl was less certain. There ensued the immemorial argument. That boy had not learned how to command! But at last she said "yes". On the day when we all have to take account for our actions before our Creator, I shall take upon myself that young lady's indiscretions, for I desired it even more ardently than did her suitor.'

At last the boy won his point and the couple left. Mendès-France slid down the wall and left for the railway-station and freedom.

There is a charming sequel to this story. Mendès-France did not forget the unwitting heroine. When he returned to France after D-Day, he sent her an open letter saying:

'I do not know what you said "Yes" to that night, but if you did something that a young girl shouldn't, then I shall plead for your forgiveness more passionately than if I were your lover.'

Maybe today the name of Mendès-France means little. But he escaped to join the Free French and he took part in bombing missions to France and Germany. He must surely have been the first Prime Minister in history to have bombed the capital of his own country. This occurred when the target was an electricity transforming station in Paris.

For the record Mendès-France was Prime Minister for less than a year. But he was a man in just as much of a hurry then as when he escaped from prison. He made himself intensely unpopular by telling the French how much they needed to pull themselves together. He gave independence to Tunisia and to French territories in India. He ended the war in what was then Indo-China and later became Vietnam. Had Mendès-France remained Prime Minister it is doubtful if even America would have allowed herself to be dragged into one of the most futile wars of modern times.

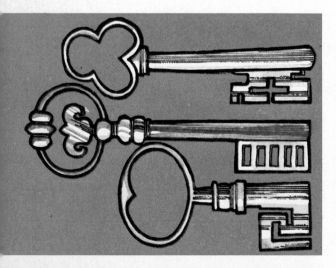
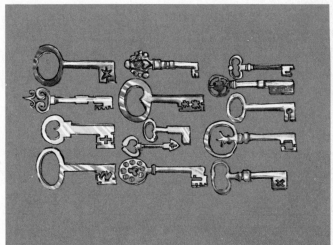
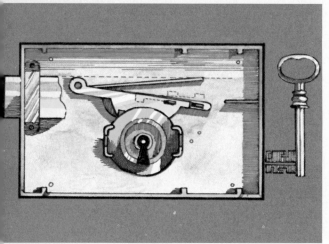

Chapter 3

A matter of keys and handcuffs

For many years the chief problem facing the would-be escaper from a prison was simply a matter of stealing, borrowing, copying or finding the right key.

The prisons of earlier years, both military fortresses and civilian prisons, were mainly massive stone-built buildings with strong iron bars round the high, narrow windows, far stronger and tougher to negotiate than those through which Pierre Mendès-France managed to file.

Now unless a prisoner was himself a locksmith, or knew how to pick a lock, he depended greatly on help from outside. It was then that his pals really counted. Their job was to find a locksmith. In nearly all cases the planning of such escapes involved the study of keys and locks which eventually became a vital technique in the art of escapology.

In 1873 there was an outcry among the public, mainly incited by indignant editorials in the local newspapers, about the large number of escapes from Sing Sing Prison in New York. Local politicians demanded action and a team of detectives was set up to investigate the mystery of how so many prisoners managed to get away from a prison intended to hold dangerous criminals.

For a long time the investigating team had no luck at all. Word had gone round that inquiries were being carried out and the original underworld had their own code of silence and deception.

Then Mary Moon was arrested for shop-lifting. Her room on Third Avenue, near Fifty-Second Street, in New York, was searched and the detective came across a suspicious-looking tin box which was hidden in the drawer of a desk. When the box was opened the detective found inside it, carefully wrapped in tissue paper, the wax impression of a large key.

Sing Sing Prison

A thorough check was made and eventually the detectives' team discovered that this wax impression resembled the key which unlocked the doors in Gallery No 19 at Sing Sing. It was quickly obvious that 'Long Mary Moon', as she was known, was the jail-birds' chief accomplice. Her one fatal mistake was to be greedy and indulge in shop-lifting at a time when all the Sing Sing escape plotters needed to lie low. The detectives made a list of all her friends and found that one was John Steurer, a German locksmith. Detectives went to his workshop, pretended to be burglars who needed his assistance and finally trapped him and ended the escape network.

On the morning of 19 November, 1873, a young and pretty girl stood outside the iron gate which admitted visitors to Tombs Jail in New York. At ten o'clock promptly the gate swung open. The warders knew the girl well as a regular visitor and did not search her as thoroughly as they might have done. A pretty face can often be an excuse for laxity. So Maggie Jourdan, taking advantage of the fact that it was quite normal to muffle up heavily on a chill winter's morning, got her ticket to visit the prisoner, William Sharkey, in his cell without any difficulty. She carried on her person a spare dress and went straight to Cell 40.

Incarcerated in this cell, which was regarded as being guaranteed to keep the toughest criminal secure, was William J Sharkey, a man who was not only a pickpocket and a petty thief but also a bank raider, a politician of corrupt influence and the murderer of Robert S Dean, on which charge he was being held in prison at that moment.

Maggie Jourdan was able to slip the spare dress through the bars of the cell and, at the same time, she passed to William Sharkey the key which she knew would operate the lock perfectly.

A quarter of an hour later another woman came from the prison corridors and gave up the usual visitor's ticket. She wore a dark, woollen dress, black coat, Alpine coat and a thick green veil.

Then, an hour later, another woman walked out, was asked for her ticket and searched. She said she must have lost it. An immediate alarm was given, all the cells were searched and Sharkey was found to be missing.

Maggie Jourdan had taken an impression in wax of the key of her lover's lock the day before he escaped. She was arrested for trying to help Sharkey escape, but the jury failed to agree on a verdict and so she was acquitted. It was said at the time that Maggie charmed the jury just as she had always charmed the warders.

It is not known to this day where Sharkey went after his escape. He certainly had no intention of rescuing Maggie

Jourdan. He probably lay low in New York for a while and
then went by ship to Cuba.

At any rate two years later he was joined in Havana
by Maggie Jourdan, who was devoted to him considerably
more than he was to her. Alas, as the New York chief of
Police, George W Welling, reported afterwards, 'The girl's
devotion was poorly rewarded. With base ingratitude he
(Sharkey) soon began to ill-use her and eventually she left
him and returned to New York'.

But even in these tough days nothing deterred the would-be
escaper. If a key could not be waxed and re-cut, if accomplices
could not be found, alternatives were sometimes, though
admittedly rarely, possible. It all depended on how small the
prisoner was.

From Tombs Prison in New York twenty-eight people
escaped in 35 years, but most of them had to use considerable
ingenuity, especially when the lock could not be picked, or a
master-key supplied by an accomplice.

In July, 1860, Conrad Smith with two other prisoners was
confined in a cell on the second floor. There was no hope of
picking a lock, or getting a master-key smuggled in, so
Conrad, a lithe, slim individual with a good deal of agility and
a contortionist's talents for wriggling himself into almost
impossible positions, developed a new technique for escape.

He removed the iron lintel from under the window, leaving
an aperture of 29 inches long and $6\frac{1}{4}$ inches broad. Having
achieved this modest effort at a very narrow opening, he
soaped himself all over from head to foot and then managed
to wriggle through the small space.

Dropping to the ground below, he climbed to the roof of
the cookhouse, which was at the rear of the prison. The top
of the outer wall was 30 feet from where he stood, but
somehow he got up on it and then jumped to the street, a
free man. He was only at liberty a month, however, having
been recaptured in a beer saloon on the Bowery.

One of the subtlest plots involving escaping by obtaining the
right key was that concerning the rescue of Eamon de Valera,
former President of the Irish Republic, from Lincoln Jail in
England in February, 1919.

Eamon de Valera was always noted for his political
stubbornness. His enemies said he showed what an
impossible man he was to deal with; his friends believed that
it was this very obstinacy, refusal to budge an inch that not
only resulted in the Irish gaining their independence, but, by
refusing the British the use of their ports in wartime, saved
Ireland from being invaded by the Germans in World War II.

Whichever view you take, it is certainly clear that it was
his stubbornness, patience and careful planning that enabled
him to escape from prison.

Like many fervent Nationalist rebels he came from mixed stock and was not even born in Ireland. His mother was Irish, but his father was a Spaniard who had emigrated to the United States where he was born in New York in 1882.

After his father's death he returned to his mother's country, where he was educated and where he gradually took up the cause of those fighting for freedom from Britain. As a leader of the Nationalist rebels he had a chequered career, sometimes being forced into hiding, at other times boldly making revolutionary moves against the British occupying forces.

He was commandant of the notorious Easter Uprising in 1916, was sentenced to death by the British, but had his sentence commuted to penal servitude for life. Then he was released in the general amnesty of June, 1917. The same year he was elected Sinn Fein Member of Parliament for East Clare.

Eamon de Valera

It was a short-lived triumph. Though the Republicans had won many seats in the election, many of those who had won seats were held in British jails. De Valera was among them: he was shut up in Lincoln Prison on the eastern side of Britain far from his beloved Ireland.

He was, however, quite determined to escape and to that end spent day after day thinking up ways and means. As with so many other prisoners his mind revolved around the need to get hold of a key.

De Valera was a Catholic and as such had access to the prison chapel. He felt sure that if he kept his eyes open one day when he went to mass he would get a glimpse of where the chaplain kept the pass-key, which he must possess.

Thus, one Sunday morning, going early to mass, De Valera saw the pass-key lying in the sacristy. There were now two problems to be solved: first, would the pass-key generally be

A party of Sinn Feiners marching through Dublin under escort, Easter 1916

left in this place (it was tucked away in a place where nobody but so vigilant a man as De Valera would spot it); secondly, how could he get a wax impression made of it?

The answer to the first problem depended on the habits of the chaplain; whether he was a methodical man, or if he left the key in different places. But the second problem was much easier to solve. De Valera rummaged around for some wax candle-ends which had been discarded from the candle-sticks. He put them in his pocket and hid them in his cell.

Waiting until the following Sunday, De Valera melted the candle-ends and, keeping them warm against his body, made his way to the chapel and went into the sacristy. There he found the key and swiftly made a wax impression.

That was a start, but the next problem was how to get a key made from the wax impression. Nobody in Lincoln Jail could help him. His only chance was to get aid from Ireland.

A group of prisoners after the Easter uprising

Perhaps it was that original and peculiar Irish sense of
humour and imagination which stood him in good stead. The
Irish have a great memory for comic songs, especially for
songs about drunken men. They tell more funny stories about
drunks than any other nation in the world.

One such ditty ran through his mind:

'There he was, outside in the rain,
All the Irish whiskey fuddling his brain.
He tried to get the latch-key in,
But every time he missed.'

Those weren't quite the exact words of the song, but they
were enough to give De Valera an idea of what to do next.
One of his fellow-prisoners was good at making amusing
sketches and De Valera persuaded him to draw two pictures of
another prisoner, Sean McGarry.

Each picture was drawn on a postcard. The first showed
McGarry, drunkenly trying to get his latch-key in the door of
his Dublin home. The caption was 'Christmas, 1917: he
can't get in.' The second card showed McGarry sitting
gloomily in his cell, his face staring at a large key-hole in the
door and the caption here was: 'Christmas, 1918: he can't get
out.'

To most people these cards would have meant nothing at all.
They would have seemed like some kind of sick joke at a poor
prisoner's expense. But the artist was more than a slick
sketcher; he was a skilled draughtsman and what he had done
was to make the key and the keyhole the exact sizes of the
pass-key and the actual keyhole. The rest of the picture was
in miniature. In other words, the two amusing sketches
contained a carefully measured replica of key and keyhole
carried out from the wax impression.

One final question remained: would the Irish agents at the
other end be quick-witted enough to grasp the importance
of the two postcards which were given to an unsuspecting
warder to post to McGarry's wife in Dublin. To the English
warder it was just typical of these 'mad Irish jokers' with their
peculiar sense of fun.

'I'll post them for you,' he said gruffly, but not unfriendly,
'but I'm damned if my wife would see the funny side of these
pictures. At least she wouldn't if *I was the one* in prison
writing to her.'

'Oh, she has a sense of humour,' was McGarry's reply.
'She'll laugh her head off.'

There are two versions of this story of the postcard message
and probably only Eamon de Valera himself could confirm
which was the correct one, if indeed he remembers, as he is
well into his nineties today.

One version has it that the two sketches were on one
postcard; the other was that there were two separate postcards.
I am inclined to believe the second version as the idea was

that McGarry's wife would show both pictures to his pals and that they would start comparing them. Also I doubt if even a skilled draughtsman could get so much accurate detail and life-scale measurements on a single postcard. There is just one other possibility; that the card was an especially large one, but I think they would have ruled this out on the grounds that its very size would have drawn the attention of the authorities to the fact that something odd was going on.

The success of the operation depended upon McGarry's wife letting as many rebels see the postcards as was possible in the hope that one at least would read the hidden message.

Luckily one or two of the brainiest and quickest-witted members of the Irish Republican Army had by then got out of jail and they were among those to see the sketches.

One of these was Michael Collins, Intelligence Chief of the IRA, one of the most brilliant and daring minds in the whole movement. He not only had a great sense of fun, but was quick to spot an intended message.

'Look,' he cried excitedly, 'there is more than just a cheerful joke in these sketches. That key is life-size: the details are carefully measured. It must have been copied from a wax impression of the original key. And look at that key-hole: it must be the size of the real key-hole to their cell, or some other vital door. Why would they put such minute detail at such size into miniature sketches where the figures are almost smaller than the key? Get that photographed at once. I know Dev. He's as cute as an Irish hobgoblin on a night out around the Liffey and just as fanciful in his ideas. He is trying through McGarry to give us a picture of the key he needs to escape.'

Plans were immediately launched to rescue De Valera and his friends from Lincoln Jail. Frank Kelly was detailed to go to Lincoln, live there and keep a watch on the jail. For weeks he had very little luck, but gradually he met a few warders in the city's public houses and got talking to them. It was a risky process as there was every chance that one of them would become suspicious and Kelly would be arrested.

Finally Kelly made a contact with the catholic prison chaplain and asked him to pass a message to one John O'Mahony in Lincoln Jail. It was an innocent-enough message but Kelly felt sure that O'Mahony would guess that a rescue attempt was to be made.

In the meantime a key-maker in Dublin had made a replica of the key from the postcard. Michael Collins warned that the probability was the key wouldn't work.

'Why not?' indignantly asked the key-maker.

'Well, you see now, how do you usually make an accurate copy of a key?'

'Why, from the key itself, of course.'

'Exactly. And sometimes you find an angry customer comes back and says it doesn't work.'

Michael Collins

Relatives visiting prisoners after the Uprising

'Very occasionally.'

'Nevertheless it does happen, especially with a tricky key. But here we don't have the original key, we don't even have the original, somewhat amateurish wax impression of that key. We just have a sketch of the impression.

'We are a very long way from success yet. First we must send in this key and see if it works. If it is intercepted, or if it doesn't work, it won't matter a great deal. But we must aim to get a perfect key made as soon as possible and not just rely on this first effort.'

The replica of the key drawn on the postcard was put inside a cake which Mrs McGarry had baked and was sent to her husband in Lincoln Jail. They did not risk sending the cake by post, but gave it to another agent, Fintan Murphy, who handed it in at the main gate of the prison to a warder.

The latter appeared to be suspicious at first and took out a knife and poked about in the cake. 'Ah, well,' he said, 'it's home-made and it looks good' and, without cutting any more, sent it in to the prisoner.

But this time they were unlucky. McGarry extracted the key from the cake, put it into one of the cell doors and it broke in the lock. The prisoners had the devil of a job to wriggle the broken key out of the lock with a piece of wire before a warder had time to discover it.

So Michael Collins' argument and logic had been proved right. Another key had to be made, another cake had to be baked.

Nor was this the end of the rescue attempt. The agents of the IRA who had been hanging around Lincoln Jail, had at last made some contacts, passed messages in code into the prison and got replies out. De Valera wanted much more than just a key.

So a third cake had to be baked. 'But this time, begorrah,'

grinned Collins, 'we are going to put not only a key into the cake, but a whole host of gadgets with the kitchen sink thrown in.'

'And how in hell's name shall we get away with a cake weighing like a carthorse?' asked one of his confederates with a truly Irish sense of exaggerating a problem.

Collins showed the way. He put into the cake some files, a small screwdriver and other equipment, but, most important of all, some blank keys. The cake was coated with a thin layer of plaster of Paris to prevent it from crumbling into pieces. On top of it all was a hefty and very tough coating of icing sugar.

Yet even this cake got into the jail. Michael Collins moved over to Lincoln; he had all his agents placed at strategic points around the prison and the whole area was carefully mapped. On 3 February, 1919, just before lock-up time everyone was ordered to his post. Collins and another arrived at the prison. Down in the city, standing by with a taxi, was Paddy O'Donoghue, from Manchester.

The back of the jail faced a road with fields in between and along the road was a steady stream of soldiers in uniform, for Lincoln was a garrison city.

On the strike of the scheduled hour Collins flashed a torch towards the dark fields outside. High up in the window of his cell De Valera responded by lighting a whole box of matches and holding it up until his fingers were scorched.

Then, down the prison corridors, with the men escaping with him, the invaluable husband of the cake-maker, Mrs McGarry, and Sean Milroy, De Valera made his way. By now Peadar de Loughrey, another of the prisoners and an expert locksmith, had cut the perfect key from the blanks supplied. It had been an arduous way of arriving at a solution of the

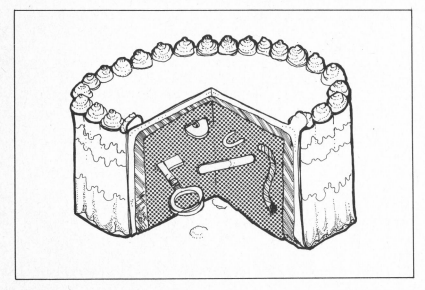

What the warder would have found in the cake

problem, but patience, allied with good humour, wit and quick thinking had paid off.

Collins had left nothing to chance: he had planned things so that simultaneously an attempt would be made to break into the prison from the outside and let the prisoners out and for those inside to try to let themselves out. Michael Collins had had a great deal of experience in escaping from the British and he always believed in what he called 'a two-way gamble'.

Well, on Collins's side this time the gamble did not work. When he put his duplicate key into the door of the back wall, it would not turn. He gave an extra hard tug and the key snapped in the lock. There were the prisoners inside within inches of escape; there was Collins outside with the handle of the broken key in his fingers.

But De Valera's master key worked splendidly. It opened not only one door, but three and enabled them to cross a courtyard into another building. From there they were able to get into a yard and reach the wall of the prison. There was the last obstacle to their success: a door in the wall. Once again the key worked. There was no doubt that Mamma McGarry's cakes had done a splendid job.

But the most galling thing of all was that Michael Collins, the master-planner of escapes, had failed at that vital final iron gate which now was all that lay between the escaping prisoners and freedom. Here his key had snapped off in the lock.

Fortunately they were able to whisper to one another through the gate and it must have been a terrible moment for Collins when he had to confess to De Valera what had happened.

But De Valera never for a single moment panicked or muttered complaints. He just pushed his own key slowly and steadily into the lock until it touched the broken end of Collin's key. One gentle push and the remains of Collins's key was pushed out, the lock turned, the gate swung slowly open and at last all were free.

They crossed the fields, got over a wooden gate and on the road and walked into Lincoln. There the taxi was waiting and while De Valera and one of his fellow escapers went off in this. Collins and the others made their getaway by train.

The planning never ceased until they were all safely back in Ireland. De Valera stopped off at Worksop and another agent passed him on to Sheffield. From there they all went to Liverpool where Collins had organised a major smuggling operation by sea. Yet it was three weeks before De Valera reached Ireland, long after the hue and cry at his escape had been given.

No mention of experts in coping with locks, handcuffs and keys in the art of escaping should omit the name of the most famous of them all – Harry Houdini.

It is not far from the truth to say that Harry Houdini, without even knowing it, laid the foundations of the escapology escapes which became essential in the latter stages of World War II.

The trouble was that though Houdini was a celebrity in the early days of the century, a legend in his own life-time, most people just did not take him seriously. He could have saved many lives in World War I simply by organising escapes, if only the authorities had consulted him.

But they were stupid, unimaginative and believed that Houdini was part crank, part phoney and part supernatural. This was a very foolish assessment, because he had studied the arts of escape over a long period, made himself into an absolute professional, albeit a showman, and there was many a trick to be learned from him.

The trouble with Houdini was that he was a showman, first and foremost. He liked to create the impression that he was a magician, who could perform feats beyond the talents of ordinary men and women. His legendary leaps from bridges while handcuffed, the way he managed to escape from nailed and roped boxes, sometimes submerged under water, made him into one of the most sensational and popular artists of the music hall of his age.

In the beginning it was hard going. Everyone suspected him. His challenges were contemptuously accepted. But he left behind him a wealth of detail of exactly how he made an art of escapology.

As early as 17 March, 1904, Harry Houdini had an audience of 4,000 at the London Hippodrome. The *Illustrated Mirror* had challenged him to escape from what were described as 'the strongest pair of handcuffs ever made. The Manacles had six sets of locks and nine tumblers in each cuff. A Birmingham man had laboured five years and used a vast amount of expensive equipment to make them'.

There was in fact a determined attempt to prove Houdini to be a fake and mere illusionist. No doubt Houdini ruefully thought, 'Well, every escaper must have his bit of luck', but he took it in good part.

The handcuffs were closed on Houdini's wrists. A key was inserted and turned in each keyhole.

Houdini was for once modest: 'Ladies and gentleman,' he said. 'I am now locked up in a handcuff that has taken a British mechanic five years to make. I do not know whether I am going to get out of it or not, but I can assure you I am going to do my best.'

Thus manacled, Houdini bent down and crawled into his small black cabinet. He was surrounded by observers. Then

HARRY HOUDINI THE JAIL BREAKER
INTRODUCING HIS LATEST & GREATEST
PRISON CELL & BARREL MYSTERY

HOUDINI is strapped & locked in a barrel placed in a police cell which is also locked and in less than 2 seconds changes places.
£100. WILL BE PAID TO ANYONE FINDING TRAPS, PANELS OR FALSE DOORS IN THE CELL

twenty-two minutes after he had vanished from view up popped his head from the top of the cabinet.

The audience thought he had already wriggled free. But he explained that he merely wanted more light on the cuffs. Once again he disappeared back into the cabinet. Then thirty-five minutes later he re-appeared. He was sweating freely, but complaining that his knees hurt.

'I am not finished yet,' he stated. Could he have a pillow to ease his discomfort? The request was granted and Houdini once again disappeared back into his cabinet.

Twenty more minutes elapsed. Again Houdini appeared. But the locks and manacles were still in place. The audience became restive. But Houdini had one more request: could his handcuffs be removed for a moment?

Perhaps you can see now the parallel between Houdini the showman and the prisoner who tries to escape. Each is always probing for the ultimate clue for the breakaway.

The representative of the *Illustrated Mirror* was in a quandary. He knew that if Houdini had his cuffs opened, he would see how it was done, and he had already seen how they were put on.

'I regret, Mr Houdini, but I cannot do that unless you will admit you are beaten.'

But Houdini refused to be beaten. A contemporary reporter described how he shook his head, twisted his hands round so that he could reach a pocket-knife in his coat pocket. He pushed this up to his mouth, opened the blade with his teeth. Then he went into considerable contortions so that he could force his coat over his head until it was inside out between his manacled, padlocked hands.

The first step in this 'roped-to-a-chair' escape was to tilt it over

With knife between his teeth he slit the coat into ribbons and once again went back into his cabinet. The best part of an hour went by while the orchestra played tunes to keep the

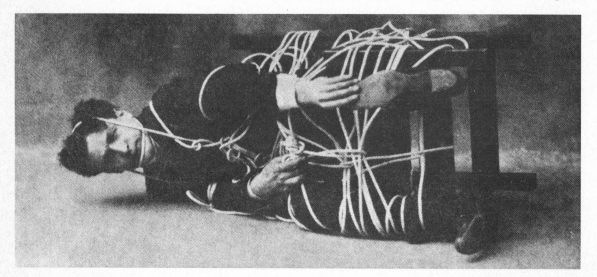

audience from boredom. Then, supreme artiste that Houdini was, he suddenly jumped out of his cabinet. His hands were free and he held the padlocks above his head.

Nobody has ever given an absolutely satisfactory solution of how Houdini escaped. But then, for that matter, we only know part of the story of how De Valera escaped. Some writers have suggested that fraud was practised and that somehow his wife persuaded the newspapermen to let her have the key to the padlocks which she passed to him in a glass of water. But there is no contemporary account to confirm this. It smells of malice among his detractors.

Milbourne Christopher, Houdini's biographer, writes that 'more than forty years after his last performance in 1926, Houdini is still the world's best-known mystifier. He created the illusion that he could squeeze through the keyhole of a lock. No manacle, straitjacket, or jail could hold him. He was, and is, a symbol for man himself – the ingenious creature who overcomes seemingly impossible obstacles by sheer force of willpower'.

Showman first, he undoubtedly was. But if he had been a criminal, could any jail have held him? One has only to conjure up some of his feats, incomparable to anything performed by music-hall artists today, to realise that he was the supreme escapologist of his era.

He escaped from a sealed envelope in Chicago without breaking the paper; Russian secret police put him in a metal-lined prison van, but he still got away unaided; he set himself free from straitjackets as he struggled in the air high above city streets. Just for the record, he escaped from Sheffield Prison for a wager.

Houdini roped to a ladder

But one man saw more in Houdini than all his other admirers and not only learned the lesson, but passed it on for the benefit of escapers in World War II. His name was Clayton Hutton, who during World War I had served with the Yorkshire Regiment and had also been a pilot in the Royal Flying Corps.

He decided when World War II arrived that, though he might be much older, there was a good deal of experience and know-how which he could use in yet another war. He went to the British War Office to try to interest them.

His theme was escapology. He would show people how to escape professionally, how escapes could be organised.

The War Office viewed his enthusiasm with some cynicism and weariness. After all in the autumn of 1939 the shooting had barely started and there were very few prisoners-of-war as yet.

But Clayton Hutton played his hand carefully. He knew that his interviewer at the War Office would at least take some interest in the legendary name of Houdini and he said:

'Escapologists in particular all fascinate me. I expect it

goes back to the night I tried to outwit Houdini at the Birmingham Empire.'

And he produced the copy of his original challenge to Houdini. It read as follows:

> To Mr Harry Houdini
> The Birmingham Empire
> 29 April, 1913
>
> Dear Sir,
> When you were previously in Birmingham you escaped from a packing-case. As the case was delivered two days ahead you had ample time to tamper with it.
>
> In order to eliminate such a possibility, will you accept the challenge permitting us to bring to the 'Empire' timber, battens, $2\frac{1}{2}$ inch nails and, in full view of the audience, construct a strong, heavy box, you to enter immediately, we to nail down the lid, securely rope up the box, and defy you to escape without demolishing same.

This was signed by Clayton Hutton and other employees of his timber firm. Houdini accepted the challenge, his only condition being that the box should not be air-tight.

Clayton Hutton believed this stunt would be good publicity both for Houdini and for his uncle's timber firm for whom he was working at the time. Houdini had almost provoked the challenge by saying he would give a hundred pounds to anyone who could produce a wooden box from which he couldn't escape.

Clayton Hutton was convinced he would win the challenge, more especially as he had insisted that the box should be built on the stage in full view of the audience.

Houdini, surprisingly, agreed to everything. All else he asked was that he could visit the timber mill and meet the carpenter.

By agreeing to this, poor Clayton Hutton lost all chance of winning the hundred pounds. For what happened was that the wizard of the music halls bribed the carpenter. This was something Clayton Hutton did not discover until many years later when he met Houdini on his last appearance at the Holborn Empire in London.

And how did Houdini escape that time, apart from bribing the carpenter? Well, he gave the carpenter three pounds to nail the box together in a certain way. 'All Houdini had to do,' stated Clayton Hutton in his book, *Official Secret*, 'was to exert pressure with his feet and the end-piece pivoted on the two genuine nails. He cut himself free from the sack by

CLAYTON HUTTON TIMBER

CHALLENGE

HOUDINI

To escape from a very strong

WOODEN BOX

·WITHOUT·DEMOLISHING·SAME·

BOX TO BE ERECTED ON STAGE USING

HUTTON·TIMBER

USING 2½ INCH NAILS IN FULL VIEW OF THE AUDIENCE

At the Birmingham Empire

means of a razor blade he had palmed when shaking hands with the last man to come up on the stage – a confederate. As an expert escapologist, he had no trouble in slipping out of the handcuffs.'

But, as we shall see later in this book, Clayton Hutton may have lost his challenge, but the very experience gained him a remarkable job in World War II.

Chapter 4

Bizarre escapes

It is generally reckoned that of all countries in the world from which to escape Russia is probably the most difficult. Nor is this just a modern phenomenon: it was much the same, though perhaps not quite so hazardous, during the days of the Czars.

Mention of Harry Houdini recalls one bizarre escape which caused the Russian police to carry out a drastic overhaul of precautions to prevent prisoners from escaping, especially those who were being exiled to Siberia.

It was in 1903 that Harry Houdini arrived in Moscow to put on a show. From the beginning it was made very clear to him that his presence was not exactly welcome. 'You had better watch your step,' the chief of police, Lebedoev, told him. 'I have total powers over all theatrical and music hall acts in Moscow and I can change programmes as I wish. What is more I can order you to leave Moscow in twenty-four hours, if I so desire.'

Houdini was fascinated during the early days of his stay in Moscow by the travelling prisons – jail vans, drawn by horses, which conveyed prisoners banished to Siberia. He was horrified at the conditions in which these wretched people were herded together, but, observant as ever, he made some mental notes on the construction of the wagons.

Escape seemed almost impossible. Certainly the top, front, bottom and sides of the wagon offered no way out. But Houdini noticed that at the back there was a door fastened by a single padlock and above this a tiny, barred window.

Lebedoev's arrogance and attitude had annoyed Houdini, but he decided to play up to the police chief. He went to him and volunteered to try to escape from one of these travelling jails. If he did not succeed, well, Lebedoev would probably feel pleased with life and be more tolerant toward his acts; if he did succeed, well, his publicity in Moscow seemed assured.

Suspended upside down in a strait-jacket in Washington

Minutes later, he was free

The Russian police chief agreed to let Houdini make the attempt, but had him stripped and searched before he was allowed into the prison wagon. The police put fetters round his ankles and two iron bars, linked by a short metal bar effectively padlocked his wrists. Then he was locked in the wagon.

It took Houdini twenty-eight minutes to free himself. At first the police were astonished and incredulous. Then surprise gave way to anger. When Houdini asked Lebedoev if he would sign a statement, confirming that he had escaped from a travelling jail, he indignantly refused.

'It would be more than my job was worth,' he told Houdini. It probably would have been, but nevertheless the news quickly spread through Moscow of what Houdini had achieved and his popularity was such that he was able to extend his booking for eight weeks.

How did Houdini make this bizarre escape from one of the most impregnable jail-wagons in Russia, surrounded as it was by police who were actually prepared for an attempt at escape? One British writer, J C Cannell, has suggested that Houdini cut through the floor of the transport cell, removed the wooden plank beneath and then slipped out.

Houdini left no explanation in his private papers, but the foregoing theory seems improbable. There is, however, a clue in the lithographed sketch of the prison-wagon which the great artist used in his advertising. This sketch shows the tiny window above the door at the back of the van. But, if one compares this with a photograph of a real prison-wagon, it is clear there are marked differences.

In the sketch Houdini used the window is tinier than it really was and much higher above the padlocked door. In fact, if one studies a photograph of the real prison wagon it is clear that the only possible way of escape would be for Houdini to stretch his arm through the barred window, reach for the lock and pick it open. But Houdini was anxious to disguise his actual method of escape.

The Lord prepared a great fish to swallow up Jonah. And Jonah was in the belly of the fish three days and three nights. Then Jonah prayed unto the Lord his God out of the fish's belly and said, '. . . I am cast out of thy sight; yet I will look again towards thy holy temple . . .'
And the Lord spoke unto the fish and it vomited out Jonah upon the dry land.

We all know the Biblical story of perhaps the strangest escape of all time and how Jonah spent three days and nights in the belly of the whale. What is not so generally known is that an escape from the belly of a whale has also occurred in more recent times.

**'And the Lord spoke unto
the fish and it vomited out
Jonah upon the dry land'**

Nor is this just the yarn of a leg-pulling sailor. It was
checked, verified and documented and finally published as a
factual account in the *Journal des Débats* of Paris on 14 March,
1896.

So macabre and fantastic was this story that it took nearly
five years' checking of the facts, re-examining witnesses and
obtaining medical evidence before M Henri de Parville, the
science editor of this highly serious newspaper, was able to
accept it as authentic.

The whaling ship *Star of the East* was far out in the
Atlantic Ocean on 25 August, 1891, when she sighted a large
school of sperm whales. Immediately whaling-boats were
launched with the object of getting close to propel lances
against the whales.

One whaling boat had moved in rather closer than was wise
against these enormous and quite ferocious whales. A lance
had been hurled at a whale, wounded it, but also caused it
to swoop down on the boat in a sudden, lashing attack.

The whale fixed its powerful jaws on to the whaling-boat
and crushed it. Like matchwood under the force of the huge
whale, the boat disintegrated, throwing the sailors into the
ocean.

Helmsman James Bartley, who was in charge of the boat,
had held on just a few seconds too long in the hope of avoiding the whale's headlong attack. While the rest of the crew
jumped to comparative safety in the sea, poor Bartley found
himself leaping into the open jaws of the whale.

With gasps of horror the other sailors saw Bartley disappear
inside the whale. They assumed that was the end of their
shipmate and they turned away and swam in the direction of
another whaling-boat. Eventually they returned to their ship.

The *Star of the East* cruised around these waters for several
hours as the captain felt sure that probably at least one, and

possibly two whales had been sufficiently wounded by lances for them to be killed off eventually. The captain of the ship also knew that sperm whales can not only dive for considerable depths – as deep as several thousand feet, but that they can remain below at great depths for up to an hour or more.

Patience rewarded the whalers. At last the huge hulk of a dead sperm whale came to the surface. It was hauled alongside and for two days the crew removed its blubber.

Then one of Bartley's crew-mates suggested that this was possibly the very whale which had swallowed the unfortunate helmsman. After some argument it was agreed that, in an effort to find Bartley's corpse, and to give him a decent burial at sea, the stomach and intestines of the whale should be opened up.

Suddenly there was a roar of astonishment from one of the seamen: 'My God! There's a body inside this whale and it looks as though it's human and intact!'

'Impossible,' replied his mate. 'Why we actually saw that whale's jaws close on Bartley as he fell into its mouth. He must have been turned into pulp almost immediately.'

'Well, look at this,' retorted the other, hacking away at the intestines with his knife.

There, through the membranes of this whale's enormous stomach could be discerned the outline of a man. Instinctively the sailors started to use their knives more carefully, slicing away the skin and muscles so that they should not mutilate what they now took to be their comrade's dead body.

It was Bartley all right. But he was not dead, though unconscious. They carried him up to the deck of the whaler, hardly daring to believe that he might still survive. His body had turned a purple hue and he was covered in the blood of the whale.

The whole crew got to work on Bartley. While some took it in turns to try artificial respiration, others tipped small drops of brandy down his throat, forcing his mouth open. Gradually Bartley regained consciousness, but he was in a delirium and, not surprisingly, suffering from nightmares. It took him some days to recover from his terrible ordeal. And when he got back to Britain nobody would believe his story. Some thought he was a liar, others that he was just romancing to win sympathy.

But the captain of the whaler and his crew decided that they should set down their testimony under oath to support Bartley's story. They felt that after the terrible ordeal he had undergone it was grossly unfair nobody should believe him. It was then that M de Parville came to hear of the story and became keenly interested in following it up.

This was Bartley's own description of his escape, as given to the Frenchman:

'The very moment I jumped from the boat I saw the whale

Whalers cutting open a whale turn right round so that its open mouth was right underneath me. Within seconds I felt my feet touch something soft and spongy. I knew I had entered its huge mouth and I remember going down into what seemed like a canvass covering of pinkish-white, feet first, and I then realised I was being swallowed by the whale.

'I went lower into its body and a wall of flesh surrounded me, but the pressure of this was not great and the flesh actually seemed to give way against my slightest movement or touch.

'Suddenly I found myself in what was like a tremendous sack, much larger than my body. All was totally dark. I felt about and my hand came into contact with several fishes, some of which seemed still to be alive, as they squirmed away at my touch . . . I felt a great pain in my head, and my breathing became difficult. At the same time I felt a dreadful

82

heat . . . like being in an oven . . . I believed I was condemned to perish in the belly of the whale. I tried to rise, to move my arms and legs, to shout out . . . my brain was quite clear and then, with the realisation of my awful fate, I finally lost consciousness.'

What kept Bartley alive? Probably there was just enough air circulating in the cavernous stomach of the whale for him not to be completely suffocated. Then again the warmth of the whale's body as long as it lived would keep his own body warm. Nevertheless it was an escape against tremendous odds and almost miraculous that he should survive.

There is perhaps a bizarre element in many escapes, if only in some minor detail, but the strangest escapes of all have been those in which some inexplicable supernatural or psychic element has existed.

From ancient times men who have escaped have often spoken of 'voices' which guided them, of 'divine inspiration' and miraculous revelations. Either such stories have a religious tradition associated with them, or they go so far back into the past that they cannot be substantiated, or on the other hand they proved that the escapers were suffering from hallucinations or disturbed minds at the time.

We have already seen how Harry Houdini was accused of using supernatural talents to bring about his escapes. But Houdini himself was an implacable enemy of spiritualism and superstitious beliefs. He set out openly to attack both spiritualism and those who believed he employed super-natural techniques by which to practise escapology.

The more others claimed that Houdini was himself a supernatural medium, the more he sought to use his knowledge to expose rogues who pretended to have communication with the dead. He did not openly admit to deception, but he made it quite clear that his escape techniques depended on his specialised knowledge, his studies of locks and bolts and the development of muscle power.

When challenged on why he took so long to escape – sometimes an audience would be kept waiting for twenty minutes or more before eventually he emerged from the box in which he was imprisoned – he replied: 'If I got out too quickly, the audience would immediately think that the escape was too easy. Every second that ticks by during my struggle builds up to the climax. When they are sure I am licked, that the box will have to be smashed open to give me air, then – and then only – do I appear.'

Yet psychic elements, never properly explained, have been prominent in quite a few escapes of recent times and some of them cannot be lightly dismissed.

**Commander
H G Stoker, DSO**

When such an escape concerns one man and depends on his testimony alone, it can perhaps be discounted on the grounds of hallucination. But when there are two or three rational witnesses and those witnesses can be regarded as rational human beings, the psychic element, however bizarre, must be given serious consideration.

One example of this was the attempted escape of Commander Hew Gordon Stoker, RN, a British naval officer who won the DSO, from the Turks in World War I.

Stoker was a fairly typical, rational and phlegmatic naval officer, commander of the first submarine to travel half-way round the world and to dive through the Dardanelles during the course of operations against Turkey in 1915. He had no history of any mental disorder, or what today we call psychosomatic problems, he was eventually promoted to Captain and, while starting a new and successful career on the stage in London's West End between the wars, came back into the Royal Navy in World War II. He lived until he was 81.

In other words he was a normal, disciplined human being, an extrovert and one of the last to be suspected of crankish beliefs. The test for entering the British submarine service has always been tough and exacting and is a fairly good test of a sound mind in a sound body. It was while he was in command of the submarine he was taking through the Dardanelles that his craft was destroyed by a Turkish ship and he was captured together with his crew.

'Beyond the fact that he was an Irishman there was nothing to make Commander Stoker different from the rest of us,' one of his shipmates said afterwards. 'He was as sound and solid as the Rock of Gibraltar, the very last man to have "visions."'

The commander was taken to a prison camp in Constantinople, where for a whole month he was kept in a dark cell in appalling conditions of filth and vermin and threatened with death if he did not tell how he got through the Dardanelles.

'I kept silent and was taken to another prison in Afionkarafhissar in the interior of Turkey. My chief companions in that prison camp were two other British naval officers, one an Englishman, the other a Scot,' he declared afterwards.

Each of these men had individually considered how to escape, but each had kept such thoughts to himself because, as far as they knew, each day might bring nearer the date of the Allies' capture of Constantinople. It was only after news seeped through to them of the evacuation of Gallipoli by British troops and the knowledge that there was no possibility of rescue from outside that the three prisoners confided their hopes of rescue in one another.

Commander Stoker became the ringleader of the tiny

escape group. He knew very little about the terrain around them and only had scant news about enemy positions between their prison and the coast. But he hoped if they could reach the coast there might be some chance of being rescued by some Allied or neutral ship.

He estimated that there were about 130 miles of desolate and often mountainous country between their camp and the sea. They would have to find their way almost solely by the stars and their chances of getting away without assistance and with no maps or adequate knowledge of the country were slim indeed. Fortunately, one difficulty which escapers face is usually balanced by an advantage. In this instance it was the fact that the Turks felt so sure their prisoners could not escape far that they only guarded the prison camp rather casually.

To get to the point of this story we will skip the actual details of their escape from the camp, especially as they managed to break out fairly easily and with the minimum of planning. The problems of Stoker and his two comrades began after they had escaped from the camp.

'We found the prison was 300 miles from the coast, not 130 as we had estimated and the sheer, stark Taurus Mountains lay between us and liberty. We tramped at night, sleeping in hollows during the day; occasionally we were able to buy food, dried raisins being our main sustenance.'

Commander Stoker explained that he had been lucky enough to retain his dispatch case containing a little money and that 'we found we could exchange cheques written on odd scraps of paper for food. So much for the Britisher's reputation for honesty abroad – even in enemy territory!'

The party set out on 23 March, 1916, when the snow began to thaw. At night wolves and man-killing sheepdogs made

Prisoners in Turkey during World War I

Afionkaraf hissar: where the prison was

every step a risky one. 'One day we saw a wolf attack a herd of wild goats and this made us realise how hungry and fierce these beasts were.

'On the second day I was taken ill through drinking impure water, becoming light-headed and delirious. I had delusions that my two comrades were pals who had been killed at the beginning of the war.'

Stoker insisted that while he was fully conscious of this delusion, in other respects his mind was clear. This hallucination – call it what you like – had its basis in something real, for, as Stoker commented afterwards, 'both the dead men were friends of mine and one was a very special friend indeed.'

The fever passed, the effects of the poisoning wore off and Stoker found his delusions passed away. Here were men pitting themselves against all the odds. Ranged against them were not only wolves and wild dogs, but the climate – hot days and cold nights – unknown mountains, precipices to cross, the unknown dispositions of enemy troops and guard posts, lack of food and the gnawing doubt that when they reached the coast, if indeed they ever did, there would be any ship which could help them.

The picture of the first few days of escape becomes some-what blurred. They had hoped to average fifteen miles a day, but had not allowed for the fact that they were all semi-starved, in poor physical condition and not even possessing a compass. You can make progress by studying the stars, but it is not nearly as easy, nor as accurate as when you have a compass.

It soon dawned on the three escapers that they had not travelled anything like the distance they expected to cover in the first few days.

'Across the mountains – the most treacherous part of the

The Taurus Mountains

trek,' said Stoker, 'we were fortunate in striking clearly marked passes. Keeping the North Star behind us, we knew we were heading in the right direction. The trek was a nightmare. We are all three terribly weak and as thin as skeletons.'

It was not until the eleventh night of their escape, high up in the Taurus Mountains, that the strange psychic influence intervened.

One of Stoker's companions stated afterwards: 'We were now at about the end of our tether. We had come so far, but we felt that with each step we knew less where we were going and that the coast was a long way off. Hunger, thirst, sheer ignorance of the terrain were undoubtedly taking toll of our mental resources. We were surrounded by high mountain peaks, approaching a narrow pass and all our instincts told us that the Turks would be guarding it at the other end.'

Nor was this just imagination. The pass was to some extent, if only lightly, guarded, watch-fires could be seen at frequent intervals and only the sound of the wind offered any cover for movements of the three escapers.

Then Stoker gradually realised that something very odd was happening. It should have worried him: he should have felt a chill fear that they were being followed. Instead it made him feel safe, buoyed up with renewed energy and strangely exhilarant.

Here is what happened in his own words: 'So that there would be a chance of one or two of us escaping should we be detected, we walked in Indian file, fifteen paces apart.

'I was at the rear of the file and one day in the distance I saw a fourth figure. He always seemed to keep a little behind.

'He appeared to be one of us – unkempt, ragged, tottering. I was too weak to wonder who he was or how he got there, or why.

PLANNED ESCAPE from TURKS —IT LED to STAGE CAREER

By Commander H. G. STOKER

(In an Interview)

This actor's real-life disguise was shaving off his beard to foil prison-camp guards— his deception went down so well he took up acting for his career.

Conscious of a mysterious fourth man in the escape party.

WE were lucky! Our submarine had been ordered to penetrate the Dardanelles, and we got through—the first submarine to do so.

But the Turks never ceased chasing us, and after several days, during an unavoidable moment on the surface, their guns got us.

The submarine sank. We were flung into the water, fished out by the Turks, and became prisoners of the Great War. I was taken to Constantinople and threatened with death if I did not tell how we got through the Dardanelles. I remained silent—and was taken to another prison in Afion Kara Hissar, in the middle of Asia Minor.

My long days of confinement were spent in planning methods of escape. Two comrades and myself loosened bars in our cells, and one night we sneaked out past the guards.

It was absurdly easy. None of the guards thought that we should attempt an escape since the prison was 300 miles from the coast, and the sheer, stark Taurus mountains lay between us and liberty. We tramped at night, sleeping in hollows during the day; occasionally we were able to buy food, dried raisins being our main sustenance.

Who Was The Follower?

I HAD been lucky enough to retain my dispatch case containing a little money. All over Asia we found that we could exchange cheques, written on odd scraps of paper, for food. So much for the Britisher's reputation for honesty abroad.

At night wolves and man-killing sheepdogs made every step a risky one. One day we saw a wolf attack a herd of wild goats, and this made

us realise how hungry and fierce were these beasts.

On the second day I was taken ill through drinking impure water, becoming light-headed and delirious. I had delusions that my two comrades were pals who had been killed at the beginning of the war.

Across the mountains—the most treacherous part of the trek—we were fortunate in striking clearly-marked passes. Keeping the North Star behind us, we knew we were heading in the right direction. The trek was a nightmare. We were all three terribly weak, and as thin as skeletons.

So that there would be a chance of one or two of us escaping should we be detected, we walked in Indian file, 15 paces apart. I was at the rear of the file—and one day, in the distance, I saw a fourth figure. He always seemed to keep a little behind.

He appeared to be one of us—unkempt, ragged, tottering. I was too weak to wonder who he was or how he got there; or why, when we stopped, he went off into the shadows.

I didn't mention him to my comrades, because I thought they might say I was suffering from delusions again. After we had negotiated the treacherous passes of the Taurus the fourth man disappeared as mysteriously as he had come.

Last-minute Capture

AT dawn we paused to prepare cocoa. One of my comrades—a canny Scotsman—remarked: "Did either of you two fellows see a fourth man following us? He seemed to be encouraging us?" We replied that we, too, had observed the stranger in the rear.

Later, I heard that Shackleton, during a hazardous trek through South Georgia, noticed an extra man in the party who acted as guardian. Why should we have experienced a similar illusion? Who was the fourth man? I have never been able to solve the problem. After 17 days' foot-slogging we were within seven miles of the coast, having tramped 300 miles. We were resting in a hollow, cooking a goat, when a contingent of armed Turks found us—within sight of escape!

Lucky Whiskers

WE were bound to pack horses and taken off to prison in Constantinople, there to await a court-martial. The formalities occupied six months; then we were called before the court to hear the verdict. All of us expected to be hanged.

There were agonisingly long speeches, which we could not understand, and endless descriptions of our misdeeds. When the verdict was announced I laughed with sheer relief. I had been sentenced to 25 days' imprisonment and my comrades to 20 days each. All the same, we were taken back to prison and kept there until the war finished, six months later!

Prison conditions were app[...] Vermin crawled over the cell[...] food was black bread and wat[...]

Another idea for an [...] occurred to me. I already [...] beard, and I thought that if I [...] it off I would not be recognis[...]

My comrades persuaded me [...] make the attempt, however, [...] ing that the risks were to[...] Anyway, I shaved and found that [...] was delighted to find that [...] my friends recognised m[...] shaven.

I told everyone in the pr[...] a newcomer. The priso[...] eager for news of home, a[...] hours I amused myself by [...] an imaginary leave to the [...] days later—after the hoa[...] discovered—an officer of [...] leading part in the [...] theatricals.

"I never acted in [...] declared.

"Nonsense," said the oth[...] saw your stunt the othe[...] that wasn't acting I'd [...] what is!"

The result was t[...] "lead" in all their [...] shows, and when I ca[...] the war I had bec[...] keen on acting to [...] professionally. I jo[...] company at Portsm[...] acted in the West E[...] owe my new ca[...] that I shaved off a[...]

'When we stopped for a few minutes' rest he did not join us, but remained in the darkness, out of sight; yet, as soon as we rose and resumed our march, he dropped into place forthwith. He never spoke, nor did he go ahead and lead us. His attitude seemed just that of a close friend who says, "Don't worry, I'm here."

'I didn't mention him to my companions because I thought they might think I was suffering from delusions again. After we negotiated the treacherous passes of the Taurus the fourth man disappeared as mysteriously as he had come.

'At dawn we paused to prepare cocoa. One of my comrades – a canny Scotsman – remarked "Did either of you two fellows see a fourth man following us? He seemed to be encouraging us." We replied that we, too, had observed the stranger in the rear.'

Their Escape Route

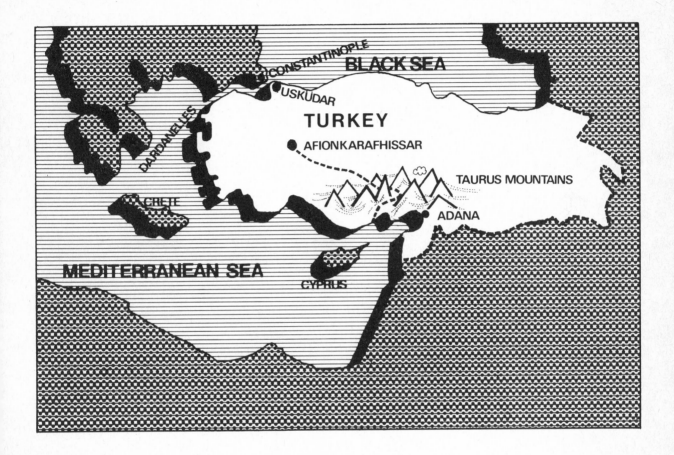

For another day their luck lasted and they headed for the coast. By comparing notes the escapers realised that not only had they all three had the same experience, but that during the period the 'Fourth Man' had been with them they had covered twice their normal distance and escaped the Turkish guards at one of the most carefully watched points on their route.

Then the 'Fourth Man' disappeared and when he went their luck went with him. They were captured by brigands, robbed and released. Then, said Stoker, 'after seventeen days of foot-slogging we were within seven miles of the coast. We were resting in a hollow, cooking a goat, when a contingent of armed Turks found us. We were bound to pack horses and taken off to prison in Constantinople, there to await a court-martial.'

It is a pity that this story is spoiled by the fact that it was a failed escape and yet, in a sense, that makes it more impressive. Stoker was not wanting to prove anything miraculous, nor were his companions, but all were agreed that something had happened during their attempted escape to make each one of them feel there was psychic guidance.

All three expected to be hanged, but after a lengthy trial Stoker was sentenced to 25 days' imprisonment and his comrades to 20 days each. But this order was disregarded: in fact they were sent back to prison and kept there until the war finished.

Commander Stoker added a footnote to his strange story. Years later he learned from Sir Ernest Shackleton, the famous Antarctic explorer, that during a hazardous trek across the Antarctic regions in appalling conditions he, too, noticed a mysterious 'extra man' in the party who seemed to act as their guardian.

Sir Ernest Shackleton: A similar thing happened to him

Chapter 5

Kings, Queens and Princes: the romance of escape

Early history is full of romantic escapes which read very much like fictional stories due to the fact that centuries ago being a king or a queen was a hazardous occupation and it was extremely difficult for such easily recognised figures to make a getaway in times of trouble without having loyal friends.

There was King Alfred, who in the beginning of his reign had to face constant threats from the Danish invaders. Once, when the Danes attacked in force, Alfred had to hide in the marshes of Somerset in an area known as the Isle of Athelney. This was not a real island, but rather a tract of marsh surrounded by a system of ditches and dykes.

The Danes avoided the area so that their invading forces would not be trapped in the marshland. Thus Alfred was relatively safe here. He had no royal robes, no money and no servants as he had had to escape in a hurry, depending entirely on the loyalty of a cowherd named Denewulf who gave him shelter in his humble shack.

Denewulf, who was eventually made a bishop, was so loyal to his King that he did not reveal the King's identity even to his wife. She is alleged to have scolded the King as a lay-about, especially when he day-dreamed and allowed her baking cakes to burn.

It was through Denewulf's cunning and his knowledge of every secret path through the treacherous marshland of Athelney that he was able to smuggle Alfred's wife and children to join him in the hiding place. Later he guided a small force of the King's followers to launch a counter-attack against the Danes, which finally left the Saxon King victorious.

When Henry I of England died in 1135 the barons chose his nephew Stephen as King even though they had promised Henry that they would make his daughter, Matilda, Queen. They simply hated the idea of being ruled by a woman. Matilda, however, had quite a number of supporters in

England not least because, though married to a Norman, Geoffrey Count of Anjou, she was part English and the great-grand-daughter of the Saxon King, Edmund Ironside. For a while Matilda went into exile in Normandy, but then David, King of Scotland, offered to help her to win the English crown by lending an army in support. Civil war followed, but though for a time Matilda's forces were successful, eventually the sheer power of the Norman barons crushed her supporters.

Matilda was besieged in Oxford, Stephen's armies ringed the city and would not allow any food to be taken into it. The people began to starve and, as much to save their lives as her own, Matilda decided to risk all and try to escape.

It was a hard, cold winter and the River Thames at Oxford was completely frozen over and all the country around covered in snow. With three servants Matilda planned her escape. On her instructions they all dressed in white with white cloaks over their faces: this, she argued, would offer some camouflage in the heavy snowstorm. Then, when the storm was at its hardest and Stephen's soldiers would be more likely to be seeking shelter than keeping a close watch on possible movements out of the city, Matilda set out.

Those guarding the gate through which she and her companions went were only too glad to let her through. They knew they would get no more food as long as she stayed. The white-clad figures then escaped undetected across the fields and walked over the frozen Thames, thus avoiding the bridges which were certain to be guarded.

Perhaps the most romantic of these early escapes was that of Richard the 'Lion-hearted' (Richard I of England) during the prolonged wars of the Crusades. While the Crusades began as a fight to maintain Christianity against the 'Infidels', as the Saracens and Turks were then called, they eventually developed into wars of plundering and piracy on both sides.

Richard was a brave soldier, devoted to the concept of the Crusades and eager to lead his forces into battle in far-off lands. On his way back home after the Crusades Richard's ship was wrecked on the shores of Austria, which then extended to the sea. Most of those aboard were drowned, but Richard and a few others escaped. Unfortunately, while he had been fighting in the Middle East Richard had quarrelled with the Duke of Austria. He knew that if he was discovered the Duke would put him in prison.

He and his party disguised themselves as merchants, but Richard was eventually arrested, brought before the Duke and sent to prison. The most remarkable part of this story is that the Duke of Austria sold his prisoner to the Emperor of Germany and the latter also put him in prison. Everybody, it would seem, wanted Richard out of the way.

The King, though a warrior and man of action, was also

Richard the 'Lion-hearted' fighting during the Crusades

something of a dreamer, a lover of music and a patron of minstrels. Years before, he had struck up a friendship with one Blondel, a minstrel, singer and composer who was a native of Picardy.

Blondel heard of the imprisonment of Richard, who he greatly loved and admired. He decided to set out in quest of him and to attempt a rescue. All he had to go on was the knowledge that the King was somewhere in Germany, as the Emperor of Germany had kept the whereabouts of his prison a closely guarded secret.

Blondel went from town to town inquiring about prisoners and, whenever he heard of an unknown prisoner, or saw a castle or jail which might be likely to hold so important a man

93

as Richard, he stood outside the walls, playing on his harp and singing a song which the King and he had composed and sung together.

'O Richard! O my king!
Thou art by all forgot,
Through the wide world I sadly sing,
Lamenting thy drear lot.
Alone I pass through many lands,
Alone I sigh to break thy bands.'

One night, outside the castle of Trifels, Blondel heard someone high up in the castle singing from a window:

'The minstrel's song
Is Love alone,
Fidelity and Constancy,
Though recompense be none.'

Then Blondel knew that he had found his King. It was Richard's voice and they alone knew these words. But it was not possible for a minstrel on his own to rescue the closely guarded King high up in a tower of the castle.

Blondel playing his harp underneath King Richard's window

In the history of great escapes women have often played heroic roles. There was the wife of Grotius, the Dutch writer imprisoned in the seventeenth century, who sent in a huge collection of books in a large wooden chest to her husband's cell.

She arranged that when he had finished with the books they were to be returned to her in the same wooden box. Instead the books were hidden in his cell and, with the aid of a confederate, Grotius climbed into the box and was carried out of the prison to be released almost immediately by his wife.

Lady Nithsdale was hardly less resourceful. Her husband, William Maxwell, Lord Nithsdale, was engaged in the Jacobite Rebellion of 1715. He was taken prisoner at Preston, sent to the Tower of London and sentenced to death the following year.

His wife pleaded ceaselessly with the authorities for leniency and organised a petition for his release, but to no avail. The Countess was not to be thwarted. Just before her husband was due to to be executed she asked to see him for the last time and for permission to bring two females with her.

Her request was granted and one of the two women accompanying her concealed an extra dress and some other clothing underneath her cloak. The two companions left the Tower separately shortly afterwards. The one who had concealed the clothes under her cloak had put on the spare dress but left behind her cloak and some other clothing. While in the cell with him the Countess did her best to make her husband resemble Mrs. Mills, one of the women who had accompanied her.

Hugo Grotius, Dutch lawyer and writer

'Her eyebrows were rather inclined to be sandy, and my Lord's were dark and very thick,' she wrote afterwards, 'however, I had prepared some paint of the colour of hers, to disguise his hair as hers, and I painted his face with white and his cheeks with rouge, to hide his long beard, which he had not time to shave.

'The poor guards, whom my slight liberality the day before had endeared me to, let me go quietly with my company, and were not so strictly on the watch as they usually had been; and the more, as they were persuaded from what I had told them the day before, that the prisoners would obtain their pardon.

'. . . when I had almost finished dressing my lord in all my petticoats, excepting one, I perceived it was growing dark, and was afraid that the light of the candles might betray us, so I resolved to set off. I went out leading him by the hand, and he held his handkerchief to his eyes. I spoke to him in the most afflicted and piteous tone of voice, . . . the guards opened the doors and I went downstairs with him, still conjuring him to make all possible dispatch.'

Together they escaped from the Tower to a house occupied by a poor woman where they were given shelter. It was directly opposite the guard-house of the Tower. 'She left us a bottle of wine and some bread . . . we subsisted on this provision from Thursday till Saturday night, when Mrs. Mills came and conducted my lord to the Venetian Ambassador's . . . one of his servants concealed him in his own room till Wednesday, on which day the ambassador's coach was to go down to meet his brother. My lord put on a livery and went down in the retinue without the least suspicion, to Dover . . . and immediately set sail for Calais.'

We have already touched on some famous escapes which have changed the course of history, but there was one failure of an attempt to escape by a British King which certainly had a considerable effect on history. This concerned that sad, devout but stubborn and in some ways rather foolish monarch, Charles I.

During the Civil Wars between the forces of the King (the Royalists) and those of Oliver Cromwell (the Roundheads), Charles was taken prisoner by the Cromwellian Army. To be fair to the Army leaders, they treated the King reasonably well, allowing him to see his friends and even offering to restore him to the throne if he would give certain assurances.

But Charles was obstinate and could not see that if he refused to co-operate he might well find his enemies taking a tougher line and demanding his execution. Carisbrooke Castle in the Isle of Wight had been surrendered to the Parliamentary forces of Oliver Cromwell and the King was imprisoned there, though still permitted to have visitors.

Several attempts were made to rescue the King and the first of these would almost certainly have succeeded if the King had not pig-headedly refused to accept a file to cut through the bars of his window. He insisted that he was small and slim enough to squeeze through the bars when his rescuer arrived below.

His friends had planned well. They had a team of helpers with fast horses waiting at key points to take Charles to a boat which was to ferry him away to safety. A man waited below his window at the appointed hour and another, from a distance held aloft a lantern to signal that all was ready.

For several minutes the man beneath Charles's window impatiently and anxiously watched for signs from his King. The longer he had to wait the greater danger he was in from

Carisbrooke Castle, as it was in the eighteenth century

arrest by the patrolling guards. Then came the King's light signal from the window that he could not squeeze through the bars.

That stubbornness on Charles's part eventually cost him his life. He was beheaded outside the Palace of Whitehall on January 30th, 1649.

His son, Prince Charles (he ultimately became King Charles II, the 'Merry Monarch') was luckier, probably because he was less stubborn and heeded advice. After his father was executed by decree of Parliament, young Charles had himself proclaimed King of Scotland and, with a small Scottish force, marched to England where, at the Battle of Worcester, he engaged Cromwell's Parliamentary forces and was outnumbered and defeated.

Charles was only a short distance ahead of his pursuers when he left the battlefield. Cutting off his hair, staining his face and hands brown and wearing coarse, patched clothes instead of silks and satins, he looked like a labouring man and, with an axe over his shoulder, disappeared into the woods, pretending to be a forester.

Charles II

The Tower of London

He headed north-west from Worcester and soon found that, with Cromwell's soldiers searching for him everywhere, he was not safe in one place for long. There were six brothers named Penderell, who were all told of the King's need to escape, and each loyally helped Charles with his disguises, changes of clothing and hiding places. Posing as wood-cutters, they guided him away from searching soldiers and hid him in a hay-rick one night.

From Worcestershire the Prince came to Shropshire and here he encountered still more soldiers. Fortunately he spotted them at a distance and was able to climb up into the branches of an oak tree unseen.

'In this wood I stayed all day, without meat or drink,' he wrote afterwards, 'and by great good fortune it rained all the time which hindered them from searching'. It was September and the leaves were still thick upon the branches, thus giving him adequate protection.

It was lucky indeed for him that they did, for the soldiers rode by right underneath the tree within a few feet of him. Not until night came did he dare to climb down and set on his way again.

Then at Boscobel Manor House, near Shifnal in Shropshire, Charles once again had to seek shelter in a tree. There was a pro-Royalist family living in the house, but they sent warning that it would be dangerous for Charles to approach it just yet, as soldiers were searching in the vicinity. He was advised to get up into another great tree, known as the Boscobel Oak, to take with him some bread, cheese and beer and stay there all day.

The Boscobel Oak became renowned in history as the 'Royal Oak'.

At Boscobel House the Prince was eventually given temporary shelter and the lady of the manor, pretending she had to visit a friend who was dangerously ill, had Charles dressed as a servant and set off, sitting behind him, mounted on a horse. This was quite a normal mode of travel for ladies in this era, so it attracted no suspicious glances.

Eventually he worked his way backwards to the south-west, beyond Bristol down into Somerset. Several times he was recognised in spite of repeatedly changing disguises, but luck remained with him. At last he reached the coast and at Lyme Regis in Dorset found a ship's captain who was prepared to take him to France.

But escape was still difficult. At the last moment the captain's wife got to hear of the plan and she was afraid that if her husband took Charles aboard his ship and the Cromwellian forces caught him, both of them would be executed. She pleaded with her husband not to carry so dangerous a passenger.

'But I have promised on my word of honour,' replied the captain. 'I cannot let him down.'

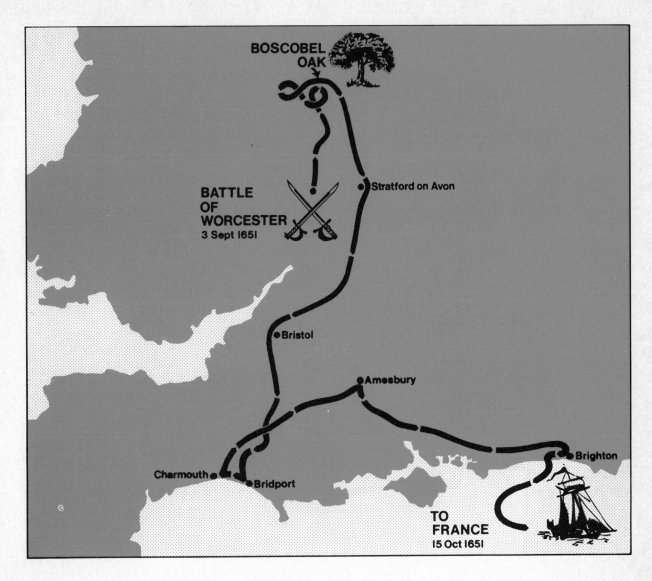

'We shall see about that,' replied his determined wife, and she promptly left the room, turned the key in the lock and left him a prisoner. She refused to let him out until several hours later.

By that time Charles, who had waited in vain for the captain, suspected a trap and had hurriedly departed from Lyme Regis. He set off along the south coast until at Shoreham in Sussex he found another captain who was prepared to rescue him. This time there was no mishap. He was landed safely at Fécamp 'after which, setting out in a hired coach, I was met by my mother, the Queen, and taken by her to Paris.'

But Charles's adventures on this escape made him vow that if and when he became King he would stay in England and 'never travel again'. It was a vow which he kept.

Chapter 6

Tunnelling to freedom

No would-be escaper has passed the supreme test of his 'profession' until he can claim that he is one of that relatively small, but proud band of men who have at least tried to tunnel their way to freedom.

When keys cannot be copied, locks cannot be picked, when outside help is lacking and all other means of escape seem hopeless, tunnelling is usually the last resort. If this fails, then all fails.

Curiously enough one of the earliest of the lone tunnellers was that romantic besieger of women's hearts, luxury-lover, spy and reprobate, Casanova, Giovanni Giacomo Casanova de Seingault.

At the age of thirty he was arrested by the Tribunal of the Inquisition and imprisoned in the Ducal Palace of Venice, accused of profligacy and practising black magic. While there may have been some truth in the first charge, it seems

Frank Finlay as *Casanova* in the BBCTV production, filmed on location in Venice

Prince Charles taking refuge in the famous Boscobel Oak

101

undeniable that much of the evidence was manufactured against him by his enemies and those jealous of his feminine conquests.

Yet, though used to luxury and the life of a gourmet and wine-lover, Casanova faced up to prison with surprising resourcefulness. We have his own story of how he tried to escape and, even allowing for certain embellishments he may have added to make the story sound better, it still makes exciting reading today.

Indeed the first part of his story rings completely true for he describes how in a paroxysm of anger, fear and frustration he pounded on the floor and walls of his cell, frenziedly clamouring to be let out. Eventually he wore himself out and settled down into a dull, silent apathy. Then he gradually argued silently with himself that his only hope lay in a state of mind between these two extremes, in other words, in quietly concentrating on how best he could escape.

Surprisingly, unlike most prisoners, Casanova's first plan was to try to tunnel his way out. He started on his own to make a hole in the floor underneath his bed. This work was periodically interrupted when he had to share his cell with other prisoners. With remarkable patience Casanova waited until he was once again on his own in the cell and then started burrowing away at the wooden floor. Days later he broke a hole through the wooden floor with an iron bar he had managed to hide in the stuffing of a chair in his cell.

But beneath the wooden floor Casanova discovered there was an under-floor of hard terrazzo. Most prisoners would have given up by this time, for Casanova had no proper implements to tackle any really tough work. Again he revealed his resourcefulness, begging his jailer to let him have some extra vinegar with his food and he used this to soften the terrazzo and eventually made a hole right through to a small room from which escape would have been relatively easy.

Casanova when he was 63

Within a few hours Casanova reckoned that he could be outside the Palace prison and on his way to freedom.

Yet he had barely got back into his cell when he was informed by the jailer that he was to be moved to another cell. Protests that he preferred the cell he was in were unavailing, but at least he managed to smuggle the iron bar into his new cell. This he once again hid in the stuffing of his chair as he knew that once the hole in the floor of his old cell was discovered his new cell would be searched thoroughly.

Casanova somehow managed to bribe or cajole his jailer into enabling him to make contact with a monk named Balbi in another cell. Casanova sent Balbi letters written with one of his finger-nails which he cut into the shape of a pen-nib, using the juice of mulberries for ink.

Casanova knew that he dared not make any more holes in the floor of his new cell. Each day they looked under his bed and scrutinised the floor. What they did not know was that the wily prisoner had smuggled his iron bar to the monk Balbi in a dish of macaroni and the latter had used this instrument to get through the ceiling of his own cell, crawl along the roof and carve out another hole down to the ceiling of Casanova's cell.

When the monk Balbi finally cut his way through the ceiling of Casanova's cell, Casanova persuaded his current cell-mate, a half-witted character named Soradaci, to cut off both their beards. He then went up to inspect the outer roof through the hole in the cell ceiling.

'Having succeeded in touching the inside of the rafters at the part where it was lowest, I perched myself on a beam, such as are to be found under the roof of every large palace.

'I poked at the rafters with the end of my bar, and, to my joy, found them half-rotten; at each touch the wood fell in dust. Being sure, therefore, that I could make a large enough opening in less than half an hour, I returned to my cell and spent the next four hours in cutting up sheets, counter-panes, and mattress-covers, to make ropes.

'I took care to tie all the knots myself, to be sure of their firmness, for a single knot badly tied would have cost us our lives. When all was done I found we had about a hundred yards of rope. There are certain things in every great enterprise which are of the highest importance, and for which a leader worthy of the name trusts no one.'

So after sunset Casanova and the monk set out on their perilous escape, though somewhat dismayed to observe how bright the moon was that night. With difficulty they climbed over the roof only to find that there appeared to be nothing to which they could fix their rope.

'I must either get away or return to my cell, never probably to leave it again; or, again, throw myself into the canal. In this predicament a great deal must be left to chance, and I must begin somewhere. I fixed my eyes on a dormer window on the side towards the canal and about two-thirds of the way down.'

Eventually this window, which Casanova only reached with the greatest difficulty, proved to be their means of gaining freedom. Casanova and the monk made their way out of the Palace, across a little square to the quay on the canal-side where Casanova stepped into the first gondola he could find, instructing the gondolier to take him to Fusina, and safety.

'Red' Leary, a burglar, escaped from Ludlow Street Jail in New York City by tunnelling through the lavatory. He was held in prison while awaiting the arrival of extradition papers for him to be taken back to Britain for a burglary at the National Bank at Northampton during the 1880's.

A short while before he escaped a 'Mrs. Myers' took three rooms in a tenement house next to the jail. About the same time two men took rooms in the third storey of the house on the side nearest the jail and then almost immediately moved to the fifth storey.

The second floor of the jail was three feet below the fifth floor of the tenement. From these rooms the men burrowed through five feet of wall into the lavatory of the jail.

Leary's cell was on the first tier of the jail. On the third tier was a corridor at the end of which was the lavatory. Leary was allowed the free run of the corridor until 10.30 p.m. He was kept posted as to the progress of the tunnelling by his wife, who, as you may by now have guessed, was Mrs. Myers. She visited him regularly and saw him twice on the actual day of his escape.

On her last visit she told her husband: 'All is now finished. Go to the lavatory tonight and you will be able to get away.'

When the warders eventually missed 'Red' Leary a search was made of the corridor. In one corner of the lavatory they found a huge hole. One of the warders crawled through the tunnel and found himself in a room on the fifth floor of the tenement house. But 'Red' Leary and his comrades had all disappeared.

One of the earliest of tunnel escapes by prisoners-of-war was the spectacular escape of 109 men from Libby Prison in 1864 during the American Civil War. James M. Wells, together with two other Yankee officers, was taken prisoner by the Confederate forces and, after a long march, locked up in Libby Prison, which was a large three-storey building lying between Canal and Cary Streets in Richmond, Virginia.

Though not built as a prison, the building was closely guarded and its doors and windows heavily barred. It was not an easy place from which to escape. A first attempt was made to burrow through a sewer, but this was found to be impracticable after much time had been wasted. Wells and his friends then decided that the only hope was to start a

Leary's escape from prison

tunnel in the basement under the east end of the building, using some fifteen picked and trusted prisoners.

This particular basement was known as the 'Rat Hell' because of the large number of vermin which inhabited it. Certainly it was a part of the prison shunned as much by the guards as the prisoners and not a place for the squeamish to work in.

Wells had figured out that if the tunnellers worked in an easterly direction they would eventually arrive under a carriage-shed attached to a large building on the opposite side of the street.

But at the very moment when this plan was about to be put into operation the guards around the basement were increased and this meant that the chances of tunnelling being noticed were greatly increased.

Finally it was agreed that the safest method would be to

A contemporary picture of the American Civil War, showing Confederate prisoners under guard of Union troops

start work behind a disused stove in a fire-place, where, out of sight, the bricks could be removed one by one until they could follow the partition wall below the floor on which the hospital wards were located.

Something like seventy bricks had to be taken out secretly at night after 'lights out' and only when this had been done could the tunnelling be started. After each night's work the bricks all had to be replaced and covered with soot and dust so that at a casual glance they would appear to be undisturbed.

Foul air was one of the greatest hazards in the tunnelling and, the prisoners having no accurate plan of the building and its surroundings, it was not easy to judge exactly when they had arrived under the carriage-shed. It was all done by guess-work and then, cautiously, and at a gradual angle, the tunnel was made to rise upwards.

Chisels and any primitive implements they could borrow or

steal were used for the tunnelling. Then, suddenly, one night the chisel of one man shot through to the surface. He knew he had reached the street because of the light of a lamp close by. It should have been the most heartening moment of all, but delight turned to cold, sickly fear in his mouth as he heard the voice of a guard calling out: 'What's that noise?'

The tunneller lay still and listened. Another guard replied that it was 'only the rats' He heard the sound of feet moving slowly away from the hole.

There was no time to be lost. A guard could easily find out about the hole leading into the street. The message went round that as many prisoners as possible were to attempt the escape, including those who had not previously been let into the secret.

It was a day of tension. Would some guard discover the hole? Worse, would the tunnel collapse at road level? Or would some talkative prisoner give away the plot? It was not until after 9 p.m. on 9 February, 1864, that the prisoners were able to make their way cautiously in small parties to the tunnel entrance.

Wells lost no time in hurrying through the tunnel and soon found himself in fresh air, making his way out through a gate into the town. Straightaway he headed for open country and kept going throughout the night, crawling into a thick copse to hide at day-break. Some days later he reached the safety of his own lines.

That less than half of the men in Libby Prison escaped is not altogether surprising when one considers that the tunnel they had created was only sixteen inches in width. But the real reason for the failure of the majority was that they behaved foolishly and stampeded in their efforts to get away quickly. The result was that some almost suffocated and were first to turn back for air, while others by their mad rush attracted the attention of the guards. This resulted in the speedy re-capture of most of the prisoners.

While James Wells was the master-mind of the American Civil War tunnelling incident, the award in World War I for initiative in this direction might well go to Anselme Marchal, a lieutenant in the French Air Force, whose plane was forced down on German territory.

No sooner had Anselme touched down than he instantly plotted a most impudent escape, speaking excellent German and pretending to the farm workers and soldiers who gathered round his damaged plane that he was a German. He even obtained their help in carrying out repairs, but was finally baulked and arrested when an observant German sergeant-major recognised the French markings on his plane.

Imprisoned at a place named Cavalier Scharnhorst, which had the reputation of being an impregnable prison, Anselme

**The exit from the Libby
Prison escape tunnel**

Marchal made an attempt to escape from there in January, 1917. He was recaptured and returned to the prison. Yet, undeterred by two failures, he spent months planning what he hoped would be a fool-proof get-away.

He decided that no prisoner would get far from Cavalier Scharnhorst unless he was able to steal or fake the uniform of a German officer, and that only by wearing this could he move about unchallenged.

There was just one snag to this plan: it was essential that his face would not easily be recognised. So all the time he was planning he kept to his cell as much as possible and, when he moved about the court-yard, kept his coat collar turned up and his face down. He was particularly anxious that the guards at the prison gates should not get to know his face.

It was impossible to steal a German officer's uniform, but Marchal and a fellow-prisoner treated their own French officers' great-coats with some permanganate of potash until the blue cloth was turned to grey. Buttons were carved out of wood by pen-knife and painted bronze, and cockades like those the German officers wore in their hats were modelled with some nickel.

Four officers were in the plot to escape: all hoped to get away, but it had been loyally agreed by two of them that absolute priority was to be given first to getting Marchal and a lieutenant named Garros out of the prison.

Marchal and Garros were in one cell, separated by a wooden partition from the next cell which housed their two fellow-plotters. They made a cunningly concealed trap-door in this wooden wall to enable them to get from one cell to the other. The main purpose of this trap-door was that when Marchal and Garros had made their escape their fellow-prisoners would slip through into their cell, get into their bunks and pretend to be Marchal and Garros asleep.

But it was immediately pointed out that there would hardly be time for Numbers 3 and 4 in this escape plot to slip out of their own bunks after the inspecting guard had looked into their own cell, get through the trap-door and into their comrades' bunks before the German guard would move into the next cell.

The solution to this problem was a somewhat complicated switch around of other prisoners depending entirely on some ingenious tunnelling. One prisoner, a skilled engineer, carved out a hole through the brick floor of one cell into the cell on the floor below, then carefully covered it over.

There was then communication between three cells, enabling a swift switch of prisoners to be carried out at night, as the inspecting guard came round, without arousing suspicion. This would give Marchal and Garros at least a full night's freedom from pursuit.

Everything depended now on the effectiveness of the faked

German uniforms, the excellence of Marchal's German and, above all, on the speed and efficiency with which the inmates of the other cells switched from hole in the floor through trap-door in the wall from cell to cell and back again.

Marchal and Garros were able to make their way boldly across the court-yard, answering the salutes of sentries and, finally, over the footbridge which crossed the prison moat. Here a crisis occurred. The escaping prisoners were asked by the sentry for their passes. Marchal decided that his best plan was to adopt the pose of an angry Prussian officer and this would suffice to silence the sentry.

'Certainly not!' he roared. 'You should by now be able to recognise me. This is the third time you have asked to see my papers recently. Do not waste time. We have important business to attend to.'

The sentry saluted, apologised and let them go without a further word.

Eventually, after many adventures crossing Germany (once they had to jump off a slow-moving train when they saw the station was filled with police), Marchal and Garros reached France and safety.

In World War II the Germans developed their own tactics to discourage tunnelling. They not only alerted their guards to scan the ground for signs of holes or disturbances, but they had dogs to sniff around on the surface. They also employed microphones to pick up sounds of digging and prisoners' voices. Once they knew a tunnel was being dug they usually allowed the prisoners to continue digging until all was ready for the escape. Then, at the last moment, the guards, holding dogs on the leash, waited for the prisoners to come out. One by one they were arrested and put into solitary confinement.

The World War II prison camp Oflag VIIC

**Captain Pat Grant
(Edward Hardwicke)
in a sewer tunnel escape bid
from Colditz**

One German prison commandant said afterwards to a British prisoner who rashly demanded to know who had betrayed them: 'You British always think in terms of traitors. You never give your enemy the credit for being as clever or cleverer than you are. We knew all about your tunnel four weeks ago. But why should we stop you then? You were busy, you were quite happy, we could keep an eye on you. We knew that as long as you went on digging the tunnel, you would not try other means of escape.

'But above all we knew that if we waited until you were ready to escape, then we should catch all who intended to escape. And from then on we could keep a much stricter watch on you.'

The best way of starting a tunnel in a German prison camp was to choose the dirtiest and unpleasantest place in the camp. The Germans themselves were hygienically-minded, almost pathologically devoted to cleanliness – a great virtue in peace-time, but a disadvantage when dealing with prisoners-of-war.

So a group of Allied prisoners in the Oflag 21B Camp in Poland agreed to emulate the feat of 'Red' Leary in escaping via the 'loo.' They chose to start digging their tunnel in the side of a trench in one of the camp latrines. One man who was particularly slim of build hunched himself together and clambered down the lavatory seat in this trench until he got to the bricks at the bottom.

These he removed one by one and started to burrow into the earth. He crawled back through the lavatory seat and reported that, providing the earth did not fall in on them, tunnelling was feasible.

At Oflag 21B a whole team was engaged in the escape operation. A certain number of prisoners was scheduled to escape; the remainder of the team (and they outnumbered the escapers) were under strict instructions only to assist in the operation.

Robert Kee, one of the escape team members from Oflag 21B, wrote in his book, *A Crowd is Not Company:* 'I myself was privileged to play a very minor role in this tunnel, acting as a stooge and keeping watch while the soil was hauled in large jam tins to the surface. From stooge I graduated to become a dispenser of excavated earth. The tunnel was a very fine one and remained undiscovered, I think because of its starting point.

'Although to the escapers went the excitement of the journey beyond the wire [fence], those who remained in camp enjoyed the triumph of the morning roll-call when 52 men were found to be missing. The inevitable reprisals followed, but they were well worth while.'

Luckily there was a mathematician among them. Not only did he calculate accurately the distances required and check what had been achieved, but he was able to prove half way that the tunnellers were digging down too deep and must climb higher to reach the surface.

Some thought fifty feet of tunnel was sufficient. The team's calculator insisted on seventy feet and, when the probing sticks eventually pierced the surface, he proved to be right. The men were able to escape outside the wire-fence.

In the years of the 'Cold War' and even up to the past few years the most spectacular escapes made by tunnellers have been from East Germany to West Berlin.

Tunnel escapes became frequent in the early days after the building of the Berlin Wall in 1961 by the Communists, but, as the East German authorities learned of the techniques used, they became increasingly rare and hazardous.

Yet on 27 July, 1973, nine East Germans, including five children, tunnelled their way to freedom into the American sector of West Berlin. This exploit was planned by two brothers, both engineers. They brought their families out by burrowing under the East German border fortifications.

The tunnel was not dug under the Berlin Wall, but the perimeter fences dividing West Berlin from surrounding East German territory. It came out beside the Königstrasse, near the Glienicke Brucke in the extreme south-west corner of the city.

Chapter 7

How to organize escapes

It was not until World War I that any real attempt was made to organise escapes and to plan them in something approaching a scientific manner. Early on in that war it was often left to civilians – women in particular – to help prisoners-of-war to escape.

There was the case of Edith Louisa Cavell, a British nurse, working in Belgium, then occupied by the Germans, who helped wounded British soldiers to escape over the Dutch frontier. A number were smuggled to freedom through her efforts, but little or nothing seems ever to have been done to protect this gallant patriot. Eventually she was arrested by the Germans, tried and shot by them on 12 October, 1915.

Her execution horrified the world, for she was not even a spy and, indeed, so extraordinarily careless in arranging the escapes of British soldiers that her ultimate arrest was predictable. Yet her example was noted and probably did much towards speeding up more professional methods of escapology.

It was not until the latter part of World War I that escaping from prisoner-of-war camps became a scientific operation and then it was limited to far less than a hundred escapes by British prisoners-of-war from carefully guarded camps across the border into neutral Holland, Switzerland or Denmark, or in some cases by boat to Sweden. A few made their way across the battle lines into Allied territory.

When World War II came, the task of Allied prisoners-of-war was made more difficult for two reasons: first, the Gestapo and the police forces of Germany had gained valuable experience in rounding up foreign workers and fugitive Jews and secondly, the choice of escape routes became much more difficult once Germany established control over most of Europe.

There was only one frontier over which prisoners could successfully escape – that of Switzerland. And, after the evacuation of the British from Dunkirk until the Second Front in 1944, unless a prisoner-of-war was held in Italy, there were no battle lines through which to get away.

After Dunkirk the need for better organisation of escapes became of vital importance. Germany had achieved the most brilliant and swiftest victory of modern times taking a large number of prisoners, and wiping out whole spy networks. The only hope of obtaining information was from escaping prisoners-of-war.

'This officer is eccentric. He cannot be expected to comply with ordinary service discipline, but he is far too valuable for his services to be lost to this department.'

This is an extract from a letter sent by the Commanding Officer of Clayton Hutton, to a Provost Marshal who obviously had begun to wonder what Hutton was doing for the war effort.

On the basis of a daring challenge to Houdini he had once made Hutton, who had served in the Yorkshire Regiment in World War I, was picked out by the War Office in London to organise escapes. He was told quite bluntly that 'one of your headaches will be the invention of new escape material.' He soon realised that neither the War Office, nor anyone else, had any conception of how escapes were to be organised from London.

Clayton Hutton's great inspiration – and it was to be that of many other escape organisers – was Johnny Evans, a man with great knowledge of the Germans and their characteristics, who had escaped from them in World War I. Between the wars he had anticipated a second war between Britain and Germany and had spent his holidays cycling in Switzerland, photographing the German–Swiss border.

Clayton and Evans got together to discuss detailed plans for organising escapes. Evans's view was that each man in all the Services should be given three basic escape aids – a map, a compass and food in concentrated form before he went into battle.

Probably many schoolboys read Evans's book and undoubtedly some of them profited from it in World War II. As Airey Neave, then of MI9, the chief escape organisation unit, now the Conservative Member of Parliament for Abingdon, told me: 'It was both fact and fiction on escape techniques which inspired one in World War II. I can only hope that another book touching on the same theme may perpetuate this theory in some future circumstances.'

Most escapers to whom I have talked stress that without having read about other people's escapes as boys they would

Johnny Evans, author of *The Escaping Club*

never have had the inspiration to try to make a getaway themselves.

Clayton Hutton was a character who liked to cut corners fast and he decided to recruit schoolboys to assist him. He collected all the vital books touching on escapes in World War I and put them into the hands of sixth-formers at a British public school, asking them to sift through everything and to note all passages which related positively to means of escape.

This attempt at a short cut was quite a remarkable success. It is not too much to say that these boys, carefully selected by their headmaster, helped to rescue an incalculable number of prisoners, for many of the more ingenious methods of escape adapted in World War I had long since been forgotten.

'A glance at the top sheet told me that the boys had taken the job seriously,' wrote Clayton Hutton. 'Everything was set out neatly and concisely under chapter headings and the salient points were in block capitals. My roving eye fell on a list of desirable escape aids – dyes, wire, needles, copying paper, saws, and a dozen other items, some of which I should never have dreamed of – and I knew right away that as technical officer to the Escape Department I was in for a very busy time indeed.'

Much of the story of how some 4,000 Allied Servicemen were enabled to escape from Germany back to Britain in World War II still remains top secret. Probably several years will elapse before it is all officially revealed. But Mr. Airey Neave, MP, has given his own account of the last two years of the war in which he was chief organiser at MI9.

'Ours was a comparatively small intelligence service so far as the number of principal agents was concerned,' he wrote in *Saturday at MI9,* 'and we have kept in touch since the war. Many of the 12,000 people in all walks of life in Holland, Belgium, Germany and other countries who served us so gallantly would have helped us again. We could have used these lines again in a third world war and were thinking of doing so had Russia invaded Germany.' This was the reason why in an earlier book, *They Have Their Exits*, Mr. Airey Neave had only been able to refer to the escape routes somewhat cryptically.

Why, you may well ask, was the title of his later book called *Saturday at MI9?* Well, 'Saturday' was the code name he adopted after he had escaped from Colditz prison camp to England in 1942. For Airey Neave, who was awarded the DSO and the MC for his war service, had the misfortune to be taken prisoner-of-war and incarcerated in the forbidding grey castle of Augustus the Strong, which towers above the village of Colditz, looking down on three sides to a sheer precipice of rock. It was known as the 'Bad Boys' Castle' because it was specially chosen by the Nazis to house all prisoners who had a record for trying to escape.

Barbed wire and machine guns bristled on its parapets and sentries were posted on the roofs. The inmates were British, French, Belgians, Dutch, Poles and Serbs, all determined to break out at the earliest opportunity.

'Every officer in this castle,' said Airey Neave, 'had but a single thought – to escape. Like all genuine escapers they conformed to no pattern. Many were eccentric and unusual men. Enthusiasm for escaping is a matter of individual character and most of us in Colditz worked out our own science of escape. Magpie boards of keys, wire, knives and useful bits of metal were concealed in private "hides" all over the castle.

'As a newcomer I played no part in the first big attempt by British officers to escape in June, 1941, by way of a tunnel which ran from beneath the floor of the canteen to beyond the outer eastern wall of the castle. They had bribed a German sentry with money and cigarettes to turn a blind eye when they emerged at the far end of the tunnel. He betrayed them and the tunnellers were led sadly away to solitary confinement.' Later the plans for tunnelling were greatly improved.

MI9, the escape organisation, did not come into being until 1941. One of its main aims was to rescue Allied airmen, whose experience was greatly needed in a Service where the number of casualties was high. Escape lines were set up to try to ensure that, once a break from prison had been made, there were people all along the routes to assist them. One of the chief of these escape channels was known as the 'O'Leary Line', which was responsible for the escape of some 600 men.

The 'O'Leary Line' was run by a Belgian, Albert-Marie Guerisse, alias Lieut.-Commander Patrick Albert O'Leary, RN. But the Germans were, of course, fully alive to the fact that those escaping were being assisted by natives of the countries through which they passed. They retaliated, and more than 500 civilians in France, Belgium and Holland were arrested. The civilians were either shot or they died in concentration camps. Treachery was one main cause of the suffering dealt out to the helpers on the escape routes. Of the 500 who died in the cause of rescuing Allied prisoners-of-war at least 150 people were betrayed by British, Belgian and French traitors who sold themselves to the Gestapo.

'In Room 900 at MI9 I was one of the two officers running this tiny organisation, a very small group indeed compared with Special Operations Executive and the Intelligence Service, yet we were responsible for rescuing this large number of Service personnel.

'I do not gloss over the early amateurishness of the organisation and our mistakes. We had our tragic moments, but there were also moments of strange humour – for example, when a sergeant-pilot was shot down near a convent and took refuge there dressed in the habit of a nun.

Airey Neave in the German uniform he made, and in which he escaped from Colditz

'He was walking in the garden of the convent looking at the flowers and made shy advances to another nun. His approach was greeted by a masculine voice saying, "Don't be a bloody fool, I have been here since Dunkirk."'

The main task of MI9 was to co-ordinate plans for helping those who were able to use their initiative in getting away from their prisons. New ideas for methods of escape, warnings on what to avoid and, above all, a supply of money, radio communications, the dropping of supplies by parachute, 'pickups' by aircraft and naval evacuations were some of the things which MI9 organised.

In neutral Switzerland there was a small band of helpers, most of them British, but some Swiss and French, who not only guided escapers across the borders from Germany, but sometimes managed to smuggle them by boat across Lac Leman into France.

From here there was an escape route, lined with helpers, which handed on the fleeing Servicemen from one post to another, from hayrick to cottage, from cottage to château, from château to midden and eventually across the border into Spain and on to Barcelona.

A key man in this network was Donald Darling, code-name 'Sunday', who set up a team of guides to help escapers cross the Pyrenees from France into Spain, sometimes sending them through to Gibraltar, sometimes across to Portugal where they would be given Irish passports. Another important figure in the escape network was Nubar Gulbenkian, the son of the immensely wealthy Iranian oil entrepreneur, Calouste Gulbenkian, and he and Darling worked secretly and effectively to arrange guides to take Allied Servicemen from France to Spain.

One of the greatest hazards to escaping prisoners in the past had always been lack of maps. Clayton Hutton decided early on that if an escape organisation was to achieve anything at all, it must provide adequate maps. Yet it turned out that at the War Office in London there was not a single really large-scale map of Germany! Hutton had to travel the whole of Britain before he eventually found what he wanted in Scotland. The question then was – how to reproduce them as easily concealed maps which above all did not rustle when opened, or crease when screwed up. Hutton realised full well that often the very moment one most needed to consult such a map was when one was hiding in a wood with enemy soldiers or police within earshot. The final solution was to have them reproduced in silk.

There were many other problems. Compasses were essential for direction-finding: disguised compasses become a matter of vital importance. All manner of ideas were developed – compasses that screwed into the backs of Service buttons, magnetised razor blades so that every razor blade become a compass.

Clayton Hutton

And as the war went on more and more inventions were added as a result of the research teams. So the number of successes grew and the number of failures decreased, despite the eternal vigilance of the Gestapo.

At the end of it all Air Marshall Sir Basil Embry sent this tribute to Clayton Hutton:

'All aircrew of the war are indebted to Clayton Hutton for what he did in the cause of escape. When I was shot down on the 27 May, 1940, I carried no escape aids, for the simple reason that there were not any . . . when I was on the run I would have given my right hand for a compass, committed a felony for a map and murder for a biscuit at the end of three days without food! It was on my return to England in August, 1940, that I first met Clayton Hutton . . . I told him my story and he described what he was trying to do to help aircrew escape. I was delighted and at once took a liking to him because here was a man of action and ideas. Some people may think he is eccentric. I think he is a genius.'

Perhaps the most professional escape organisations of recent years have been those unofficially set up to enable fugitives from behind the Iron Curtain to get away to the West. These organisations began to develop during the 'Cold War' between Russian and the Western Powers about the time the Berlin Wall was set up.

Only last year a man who called himself 'Europe's No. 1 Human Exporter', closed down his highly successful escape business and, with his wife, three guard dogs and a tame cheetah, set off for an undisclosed destination.

He was Hans Lenzlinger, a Swiss who had smuggled 156 East Germans to freedom at an average of £4,200 per head, over a lengthy period. He claimed that the East Germans had put pressure on the West Germans, who in turn put the political screw on the Swiss Government to check any further coups of this kind.

Matters came to a head when the Swiss special police searched Herr Lenzlinger's house and threatened him with imprisonment for breaking passport and frontier regulations.

Certainly Lenzlinger made the East German Government look very foolish. He would throw them off the scent by always changing his escape routes and tactics. Nothing was too far-fetched for him to attempt. On one occasion he smuggled two East Germans to the West on a miniature submarine which travelled submerged across the frontier at Lake Neusiedl on the Austro-Hungarian border.

Cheekily, Lenzlinger said afterwards: 'The submarine is up for sale. Anyone can have it. I can't use this gimmick again.'

This ace of the 'escape business' employed a staff of sixteen full-time 'escapologists', yet despite his heavy outgoings, he had a luxurious house in a Zurich suburb and his 'business' brought him in £600,000 in two years.

A bulldozer that brought five East Germans into West Berlin

Chapter 8

Escape heroes of fiction

Real life escapes can, as we have seen, be even stranger than those of fiction, but nevertheless the escape heroes of fiction tend to outlive even detectives in popularity.

Edmund Dantes in *The Count of Monte Cristo,* Richard Hannay of *The Thirty-Nine Steps,* David Balfour in *Kidnapped* and even the incomparable Mr. Toad of *The Wind in the Willows :* each one of these fictional heroes is an escape artist in his own right.

If I mention Mr. Toad, it is because he is such an improbable and awkward escaper that his very foolishness and carelessness gives one hope. In short, if Toad can get away, then there seems to be a jolly good chance that, should you or I be imprisoned any time, we, too, could copy this garrulous rascal.

But the escape of Edmund Dantes from the fortress facing the sea is in many respects the most thrilling of all fictional stories of its kind, for he had almost no hope of escaping from his cell in the closely guarded Château d'If.

Edmund Dantes hears knocking on the prison walls; he knocks back and makes contact with his fellow prisoner, the aged *abbé*. Feverishly they burrow a tunnel to link up their two cells. But the tunnelling brings them no nearer escape. The only chance that Edmund Dantes has to get away comes, ironically enough, with the death of the *abbé*.

Dantes knows that when prisoners die, they are put in a weighted sack and thrown into the sea. His only possible hope of escape is for him to crawl through the tunnel into the *abbé*'s cell, remove the *abbé*'s body into his own cell and then to conceal himself inside the sack in which the *abbé*'s corpse had already been placed. Not only had he to do all this, but to sew himself up inside the same sack, secreting with him a knife with which he could cut open the sack once it was dropped into the sea.

The chance of success was small indeed; the fact that he had to keep his wits about him sufficiently to slice open the sack almost immediately it touched the water was surely enough to daunt the courage of most men.

Thus Edmund Dantes was flung into the sea from the fortress and so he succeeded in slashing open the sack and releasing himself to the surface of the sea. And, being able to swim, he escaped.

Some authors have turned their own experiences of escape into fiction. Robert Louis Stevenson, who in *Kidnapped* tells of the escape of David Balfour in the year 1751, was in actuality reliving some of his own memories when, as a boy, he accompanied his father to some of the remoter islands off the coast of Scotland.

Stevenson's father was an engineer who helped to plan many of the lighthouses of Scotland. As a boy Robert Louis visited some of these islands and in the case of the tiny island of Erraid he found out for himself how easy it was to feel one was cut off from the mainland while with a little persistence and courage one could pick one's way back to Scotland at low tide. *Kidnapped* was the natural product of these discoveries.

Years later Stevenson told the story of how he had felt himself marooned on Erraid: 'It seemed so bleak, totally uninhabited, without any form of animal life except for birds and fish, and one had the awful feeling that here one might remain for days until one starved to death. Yet there was a way back, at low tide, across the narrow strips of sand, wading through knee-deep water here and there, but slowly, and with knowledge gained of the treacherous hollows and the friendly shallows, the way back to safety became apparent.'

Perhaps no fictional escape for sheer versatility and non-stop thrills can compare with that of Richard Hannay in *The Thirty-Nine Steps*, by John Buchan. Not only does one escape follow another, but right up to the end of the story the hero is on the run, and each escape is more surprising than the one before.

Hannay, who has returned to London from abroad, takes an unexpected and frightened guest into his apartment. He knows there is something odd about the chap and that by giving him a room he is taking a risk. But Hannay happens to love adventure and his leave in London had so far been so dull that he was ready to take the craziest of chances.

**David Balfour hides from
the Redcoats**

One night he goes back to his apartment: 'I saw something
in the far corner which made me drop my cigar and fall into
a cold sweat. My guest was lying sprawled on his back. There
was a long knife through his heart which skewered him to the
floor.'

It was clear enough to Richard Hannay that the story his
guest had told him was true enough – that there were people
after him who wanted him out of the way. But with his guest
lying dead and all traces covered, Hannay realised that he
must be No. 1 Suspect as the murderer, and that the risk of
his being arrested was as great as that of his being bumped off
by his guest's enemies.

123

You may laugh at what seems Hannay's sense of panic:
'. . . I got out an atlas and looked at a big map of the British
Isles. My notion was to get off to some wild district, . . . for
I would be like a trapped rat in a city. I considered that
Scotland would be best . . . I fixed on Galloway as the best
place to go.'

He found there was a train leaving St. Pancras Station for
Scotland at 7.10 a.m. He was fairly certain that the enemies
of his dead guest were watching the apartment block and
would be ready to pounce on him. '. . . about twenty minutes
to seven, as I knew from bitter experience, the milkman
turned up with a great clatter of cans and deposited my share
outside my door. . . . On him I staked all my chances.'

When the milkman arrived Hannay called him in and simply
said: 'I reckon you're a bit of a sportsman. Lend me your cap
and overall for ten minutes and here's a sovereign for you.'

Richard Hannay (Kenneth More) makes his getaway in the guise of a milkman

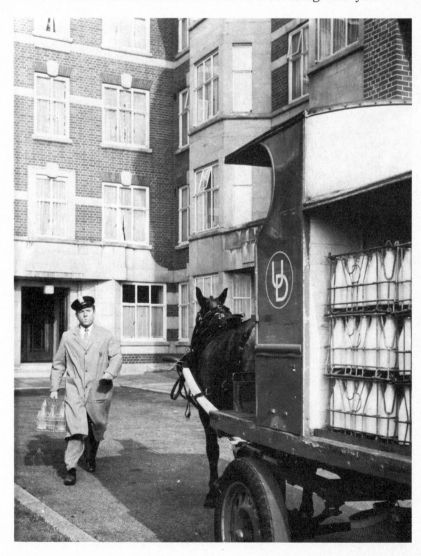

Both these pictures are from the Rank Organisation film *The 39 Steps*, produced by Alfred Hitchcock.

In his guest's pocket-book Hannay had found a few clues
as to the deadly seriousness of the events in which he had
involved himself. One queer phrase occurred half a dozen
times in this note-book – 'Thirty-Nine Steps', and Hannay
noted that the last reference to these was followed by the
words: 'Thirty-Nine Steps. I counted them – high tide
10.17 p.m.' And somehow or other the safety and security of
Britain was involved and threatened: something terrible was
about to happen which could mean war.

Thus Richard Hannay found himself being tracked down
by the police of his own country and enemy agents at the
same time. The news of his disappearance from London was
quickly dispatched to the police in Scotland. He realised that
the British police would only detain him in custody and so
ruin all his chances of finding out about the enemy agents so
he had no alternative but to avoid both.

Hannay on the run

Hannay was thus trying to escape and trying to trap an enemy at one and the same time, one of those unusual, but classic situations which inevitably make a splendid yarn. Through Highland glens and dales he dodged his pursuers – police and enemy agents alike – sometimes being trapped, but always managing to escape in the nick of time until at last he doubled back to London, confronted a bewildered and hard to convince War Cabinet and managed to get them to see that the nation's security was really threatened.

The quest now was for the 'house at the head of the thirty-nine steps' where, presumably, the enemy agents had their headquarters. It may interest those of you who like tracking down such things in real life that such a site really does exist on the low cliffs not far from Broadstairs. And, of course, Hannay found it, though not without a great deal of checking of tide tables, examining maps and cross-examining coastguards before his quest was over.

Chapter 9

From sea, jungle and desert island

Escape from the sea can in many ways be the most terrible ordeal of all. It is hard enough to pit one's wits against man alone, but to challenge the elements is something much more formidable.

We have all had dreams at some time or another of being wrecked on a desert island and living a life of idyllic pleasure from then on. There is that long-lived radio programme, *Desert Island Discs,* which envisages just such a possibility and in which you are asked what you would take with you if you were landed on such an island.

Well, Henri Bourdens and his wife, José, should be number one choice for such a programme for not only were they actually literally cast away on a desert island, but they nearly lost their lives in the process.

What is more, when they managed to wade ashore they carried a Bible, the works of Shakespeare and a battery-operated record-player with records by Bach and Mozart.

When they sailed in their 45-feet yacht *Singa Bettina,* all seemed set fair for an uneventful trip to Macassar in the Celebes Islands. They left Singapore on 20 September, 1966, and they fully expected to complete their voyage on to Ambon in the Moluccas by the end of the year.

Winds surprisingly proved to be against them, they ran short of fuel, some of their spars broke in a gale and before long the Bourdens were in dire trouble, being driven south into unknown seas.

As their food supplies became reduced they were forced to live on a meagre diet of rice, flour and sugar. It was towards the end of January that they sighted land at last and on the 28th of that month in 1967 they were driven ashore on remote and desolate Bathurst Island off the northern coast of Australia.

With supplies they rescued from the yacht before it was broken up in the heavy seas that lashed the shore, a camp of sorts was set up on this desolate island. The Bourdens spread out a sail to catch rain-water for drinking.

'We weren't too worried,' declared Captain Henri Bourdens later, 'as we thought we should be rescued before long. Luckily we did not then realise that the only habitation on the island was an aboriginal mission station about 40 miles away on the other side of the island.'

For days they explored the island, but when more than a week had passed and they saw not a single soul they began to be really concerned. Perhaps their worst and most horrifying experience was when they were trapped in mangrove swamps for three days and nights with crocodiles, snakes and mosquitoes as their only companions.

The castaway home of Henri and Jose Bourdens

Eventually they were forced to retrace their steps back to their camp. Even with their meagre supplies life in the home-made camp seemed luxurious compared with the horrors of the mangrove swamps: they had their Bach and Mozart records and for the occasional tit-bit they had sea-snails which Madame Bourdens cooked with tarragon and every other spice she had rescued from the ship.

Two months passed by and the Bourdens were now convinced they would never be found, so they decided to take their chances on a makeshift raft which they had built themselves.

But once they were out at sea they discovered the raft was slowly sinking. 'We were standing on the raft knee-deep in water,' said Captain Bourdens, 'and our main dread was of sharks. If they had come along, nothing could have saved us. I was exhausted and my wife was worse, for now crabs were eating into her sore legs.'

When they had almost given up all hope and expected to die very soon, a boat appeared on the horizon. At first it looked as though it would pass them by without seeing the frail raft. Luckily they had one smoke-bomb left and, though wet through, miraculously it worked and spread smoke on the water. Within several minutes they were rescued and taken to hospital at Darwin.

The last few years have given us some surprising epics of escape from the cruel seas. There was Dougal Robertson and his family who were adrift in the Pacific Ocean for five weeks, first on a raft and then in a tiny dinghy.

Their problem was in some respects worse than that of the Bourdens, for Dougal Robertson had a wife, a son of seventeen, twins aged eleven and a young Welsh graduate to fend for. They were so short of food that for survival they depended almost entirely on catching fish and turtles from the sea.

The Robertsons had to take to an inflatable raft, to which they attached a small glass-fibre dinghy, when their schooner, *Lucette,* was sunk by killer whales some 200 miles south-west of the Galapagos Islands.

Gradually the raft began to sink and eventually they were forced to abandon it and crowd into the tiny dinghy which had only three feet of free-board and threatened to capsize any moment.

Sharks once again were the real danger and on the eighteenth day Dougal Robertson recorded in his log:

'A new arrival came . . . a bluefooted booby landed on the sea not far away. It preened its feathers and I caught my breath as I saw a shark nosing towards the bird. To my surprise the booby, instead of taking off, pecked at the shark's nose. As the shark turned away, it flew off.

'The bird's action seemed somehow symbolic of our own defiance of the sea and its creatures and of our determination to survive in a hostile environment.'

And indeed it was typical of this family that they all sang *Happy Birthday* to celebrate Mrs. Robertson's birthday and even caught a turtle for a special birthday lunch. In really bad, cold weather they all sang to keep warm.

Curiously, the Robertsons – or rather Mrs. Robertson alone – had an experience somewhat similar to that of Commander Stoker on his escape from the Turkish prison camp. One morning she told the others that she had counted seven people in the dinghy during the night.

'She had a vision of a presence rather than a person . . . helping us to fight the storm,' her husband recorded. 'Although this was greeted with scepticism by Robin and Douglas, Lyn [his wife] maintained her belief in her vision,

The aptly named blue-footed booby

A giant leatherback turtle, measuring seven feet from nose to tail

The Robertson family at the moment of rescue

and indeed if this had helped her, then it had made a great contribution to our survival.'

And somehow it was Lyn Robertson whose spirit wrought wonders on that nightmare voyage. It was she who rubbed the chill bodies of the others when their resistance was at its lowest and she again who once took the night watch of one who was sick as well as her own.

Then on the thirty-eighth day adrift a Japanese fishing vessel appeared and rescued the whole family.

Maurice and Maralyn Bailey were saved by a Korean fishing vessel after spending 117 days adrift on an inflatable raft in the vastness of the Pacific Ocean. They had left Southampton on 22 June, 1972, to sail round the world to New Zealand where they planned to settle and make a new life.

'It was to be the journey of a lifetime,' said Maurice Bailey, 'something we had dreamed of and worked towards for nearly the whole of our ten-year marriage. We spent every spare minute preparing our 32-foot Bermuda-rigged sloop, the *Auralyn*, for the trip.'

The *Auralyn* capsized and the Baileys took to their raft, drifting 1,200 miles before they were picked up off the coast of Guatemala. They were not able to send a Mayday distress signal as they had no radio. Moral to all young adventurers who make voyages: always make sure you have a spare radio you can adapt in a raft because it is lack of communications which is usually the downfall of people who find themselves adrift far out at sea.

As *Auralyn* sinks after being holed by a sperm whale, Maurice Bailey looks on with horror from the dinghy

The Baileys also lived largely on turtles. In all they caught six sharks, thirty turtles and, says Maurice Bailey, 'over 4,000 fish. To catch fish I fashioned hooks from ten steel safety pins in the first-aid kit. We drew threads from clothes to make into fishing lines.'

But Maurice Bailey frankly admitted he could not have survived on his own. 'Our love helped us to survive all that time. It grew stronger and stronger . . . through it all we had one great consolation. We knew that if we were going to die, we should do so knowing we were completely in love.'

'We thought that it was better to die out here at sea rather than pop off anonymously in suburbia. There was never any panic. We chatted about death in a perfectly calm manner. We were never lonely. We had each other, you see . . . Maralyn helped keep me alive. There's no doubt about that. She coped incredibly well, forcing me to go on and on. I'll always owe her that.'

After the sea, perhaps the worst hazards one can try to escape from are those of the jungle.

But in the jungle the agony can be prolonged. The density of vegetation gives protection from the sun, but the fight to struggle to freedom is more claustrophobic and there are far many more dangers from wild beasts and snakes, as the couple who found themselves in the mangrove swamps of Bathurst Island soon learned.

Of one such escape – that of Colonel F. Spencer Chapman from the Malayan jungle – Field Marshal Earl Wavell wrote: 'this is a story of endurance and survival beyond the normal human capacity for survival . . . if human beings have the fortitude to bear the malevolence and hazards of the jungle and the resources to use what benefits it produces, it has no particular objection to their living in it. But the neutrality of the Malayan jungle, as Colonel Spencer Chapman warns us, is armed.

'He himself was on one occasion dangerously ill for two months on end, including a period of unconsciousness for seventeen days; he suffered at various times from blackwater fever, pneumonia and tick-typhus, as alternatives or additions to almost chronic malaria; it once took him twelve days' hard marching to cover ten miles through the jungle; and he was marching barefooted six days without food on another occasion.'

Six British soldiers who had been with Colonel Spencer Chapman in these conditions died 'not of any special disease, but because they lacked the right mental attitude.'

It was not only the elements of nature against which the colonel had to pit himself, for this was in World War II and there were such declared enemies as the Japanese and groups of Chinese bandits. Yet though captured by both the former and the latter he escaped from both and after nearly three and a half years in the jungle eventually emerged unscathed.

He has told his own story in a gripping narrative called *The Jungle is Neutral*. But to understand what he went through one must turn to other and independent versions. 'How he came through at all and still survived I shall never know,' one of his soldiers told me. 'Even though he appeared to recover in health speedily, the scars left on his mind must have lasted him all his life.'

In August, 1941, Spencer Chapman was posted to a school of guerrilla warfare in Singapore, one of the aims of which was to train soldiers to stay behind in small parties in areas which the Japanese might overrun.

By improvising and splitting themselves up into tiny groups these British guerrillas were able to cause the enemy quite a bit of trouble and also to carry out a good deal of

An aerial view of the dense Malayan jungle

reconnaissance behind the Japanese lines. There was no shortage of volunteers for these stay-behind parties, but they had to be selected with the utmost care.

Spencer Chapman felt that six was the ideal number for such a party so that they could act either in three pairs or as two parties of three. 'Alas,' he wrote later, 'how little I knew in those days about the Malayan jungle! . . . I had not realised that in the Malayan jungle a mile on the map may mean four or five miles on the ground. Nor did I realise that though a footpath may be marked on the map, it will be completely grown over in a year unless it is kept open by regular use and cutting – and our maps were more than ten years out of date.'

The torrential rain in the jungle made it almost impossible to light a fire; when the soldiers went to bed in their sleeping-bags they were soaking wet and miserable and there were so many bloated leeches feeding off their bodies

A practice assault by members of the British-run jungle warfare school in Malaya

that blood was perpetually running down their chests, arms and legs.

Sometimes they supplemented their meagre iron rations by dropping small charges of gelignite into the jungle pools and catching fish by this somewhat crude method. Colonel Spencer Chapman summed up his views of the jungle as follows: 'My experience is that the length of life of the British private soldier accidentally left behind in the Malayan jungle was only a few months, while the average NCO, being more intelligent, might last a year or even longer . . . . In this green hell they expected to be dead within a few weeks – and as a rule they were. The truth is that the jungle is neutral. It provides any amount of fresh water and unlimited cover for friend as well as foe – an armed neutrality.

'It is the attitude of mind that determines whether you go under or survive.'

Spencer Chapman had the instinct for survival plus that all important factor, the talent for improvising escape methods when normal methods are impracticable. When he was captured by the Japanese he ruefully recorded that as a fieldcraft instructor he had read every book on escaping and used to lecture on the subject: 'but none of the methods I had advocated seemed to be of much practical use now.'

After considering various ideas Chapman decided to feign a fit of coughing and complain about the smoke from the camp fire. While the Japanese soldiers damped this down he thrust himself through an opening at the bottom of the canvas of his tent. 'I heard a "ping" as a peg gave, or a rope broke . . . and I was out in the jungle.'

Dashing through the undergrowth he half fell into the river, slithered down between some rocks for a short distance, then stopped to listen. There was not a sound to be heard so he decided to follow along the banks of a stream, aiming to put as great a distance as possible between him and his captors before dawn.

Chapter 10

Gadgets, maps codes and radio: the vital tools of rescue

As we have already seen once the arts of escape become almost a profession in themselves so the aids to escaping become more complicated and ingenious and can, indeed, only be used after careful training.

The modern prison officer is not only carefully trained to watch for any slight inkling that an escape is being planned, but he is himself given up-to-date and sophisticated aids such as closed-circuit television through which prisoners' movements can be watched and walkie-talkie sets. No break-out plot will succeed today unless every precaution is taken to overcome the vigilance of the warders.

One brilliantly planned escape from Parkhurst Prison in the Isle of Wight in 1973, involving the digging of a tunnel under a workshop, failed for one reason only: a prison officer became suspicious when he saw mud on the boots of a prisoner about to take a shower.

Yet the actual plan for making this escape depended on the gathering together of a great deal of equipment over a period of several weeks – not merely spades and buckets, but vinyl floor tiles which were glued to the home-made trap-door leading to the tunnel, wood-planes, nuts and bolts, an alarm system and a whole electric light circuit of flex, bulbs and batteries.

Many of the escape aids used in World War II are already out-of-date because they are too well known to all potential enemies. Before they set out on operations over enemy or enemy-occupied territory, Allied air crews were given what became jokingly known as the 'do-it-yourself escape kit'.

This comprised such things as two passport photographs taken in civilian clothes (the idea being that if anyone was shot down over enemy territory and could make contact with one of the secret escape organisations in occupied countries, these snapshots could be utilised for forged passports).

German money, a button compass, a playing card map and a forged pass, all used in escape attempts from Colditz

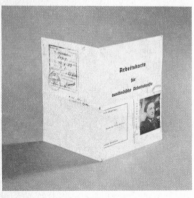

At night in France, Belgium and Holland there were always a few watchers belonging to one of the escape organisations ready to pass on the word if an Allied plane was seen to be shot down. A reconnaissance team would then go out to find if there were any survivors and, if so, to try to bring them to a hiding place before they could be captured by prowling German soldiers.

Other gadgets in the kit, which, of course, needed to be as small and compact as possible, were benzedrine tablets (to keep one awake and alert), Horlicks tablets for sustenance, chewing-gum, rubber-bag for holding water, two rolls of sticking plaster, a box of matches, compass, sewing box in a tube containing needles and thread, a map on thin silk, folded up into a tiny packet and put into the lining of the bag, and foreign currency, usually French francs, but sometimes Belgian francs, or Dutch guilders. Much later Italian currency was added.

Compasses were disguised in many forms: sometimes they were concealed in a pipe or a pencil, often in buttons. Many fly-buttons on trousers concealed compasses: they usually worked on the principle that if the top of the button was turned to the left the two halves would separate and one half contained a compass.

Of course the Germans were not slow in finding out about these escape kits. Once one was discovered they knew what to expect when some other airman crashed on their territory. For this reason every effort had to be made to keep changing the disguises and 'covers' which hid compasses, saws and other vital equipment.

Baron von Lindeiner, Commandant of Stalag Luft III prisoner-of-war camp in Germany, had this to say about Allied prisoners: 'They were always pitting their brains against our camp systems . . . This meant that in the camps we were faced with a lot of brainy young conjurors who had plenty of time in which to work out their various tricks against us.

'In the first few months we soon acquired evidence of what was going on, because after the fliers came into the camps, they were searched and found to have upon their persons the most ingenious equipment . . . Compasses of many types were discovered, so small that many slipped through a search undetected. Some of those concealed in tunic buttons were perfectly made.'

Secret codes will always play a vital part in escape aids and they are one of the best, though not necessarily the safest, means of giving a prisoner the exact plan for his escape, together with times, movements of warders and where to make for when free of prison.

A dramatic courtroom scene during Nat Greenberg's trial

But it is advisable that such secret messgages should either be done in invisible ink (for which, of course, the prisoner must have the required means of rendering it visible), or so minutely written and sketched that they can easily be smuggled into a prison in food or other goods.

Nathan Greenberg solved the problem in 1973 by writing love letters from his prison cell in Brixton, London, to his German girl friend, Erika Pijanka. The letters contained coded references in which Greenberg urged her to get a gun and stage a hold-up in court to free him.

So nineteen-years-old Erika went to West London Police Court where Greenberg was in the dock on remand and produced a sawn-off shot-gun. She struggled with a police officer and the gun went off. Another shot-gun was found in her bag.

This was revealed at the Old Bailey on 11 June, 1973, when Greenberg, a 39-years-old consultant engineer, and Erika Pijanka, together with two other men, were all accused of plotting Greenberg's escape.

Correspondence between Pijanka and Greenberg was produced in which it was alleged that references to 'Suzy' and 'Angela' meant firearms and Angela Davis, the American left-wing teacher and Black Power leader. The court was reminded that Angela Davis faced trial accused of taking a gun into an American court in an effort to free a prisoner and that Greenberg's escape bid was based on a similar plot.

George Blake

But today the use of radio communications and even walkie-talkie sets have superseded codes in all really well organised escape plans.

Perhaps the best example of this escape aid in action in recent years is typified by the sensational 'springing' of George Blake, the double-agent, from Wormwood Scrubs Prison in London on 22 October, 1966.

Blake, a British subject who had worked both in the British Diplomatic and Secret Services, was arrested in 1961 and charged with spying for the Soviet Union. He received the longest sentence of imprisonment ever imposed under English law – 42 years. Yet five years later he escaped without leaving any trace of his plans or whereabouts until eventually it was announced that he had gone to Russia.

The full story of Blake's escape has not yet been verified. There is a strong suspicion that it was cleverly master-minded by the K.G.B., though the man who has taken most credit for the coup is an Irishman named Sean O'Bourke, who had been a fellow prisoner of Blake and who, on his release from prison, vowed he would set him free.

What is clear is that a twenty-five pound walkie-talkie set was one of the main instruments in planning this escape so successfully. One must remember that as a convicted spy

Blake was regarded as a top security risk and therefore supposed to be guarded much more closely than the average prisoner. It was obviously essential that Blake himself should not only know just how close this watch was, but also be able to pass the information on to his would-be-rescuer.

For this reason radio contact between them once O'Bourke left prison was vital. But the range of the walkie-talkie set was relatively short and before tackling the problem of smuggling Blake's set in to him, O'Bourke had to satisfy himself that the radio system was strong enough to penetrate the prison walls.

Luckily, tests he carried out proved that they were. A plan was then worked out to smuggle a miniature radio set into the prison and safely into Blake's hands. The next hurdle was to make sure that satisfactory and audible contact could be made and, above all, that this radio conversation would not be picked up by security men listening in.

It must have been an anxious moment for O'Bourke as he lay on his bed in a nearby hostel, extended the aerial to its full length and switched it and the tape-recorder on.

'I set about working out our call-signs and an identifying code,' wrote O'Bourke, telling his story afterwards.* 'For the call-signs I decided to use the initials of two of the best known characters in Irish mythology: Fionn MacCuhaill, leader of the Fenians, and Baldy Canaan, his lieutenant. Thus, in the phonetic alphabet I would be 'Fox Michael' and Blake 'Baker Charlie.' As for the identifying code, that too could be on a literary theme. The first term of our English literature course had covered 'Chaucer to the Stuarts', a period which embraced the Metaphysical poets. One of these poets, I remembered, had written something rather appropriate. It was Richard Lovelace.

Stone walls do not a prison make,
nor iron bars a cage . . .

All worked splendidly. Reception was good and soon O'Bourke heard George Blake's voice coming out of the small radio resting on his chest as he lay on the bed.

Quickly and at the first call 'Baker Charlie' acknowledged the call from 'Fox Michael' and then Blake supplied the next identifying line in the Richard Lovelace poem.

Without that radio contact it is doubtful whether Blake could have been rescued. True, there was always the risk that the conversations could be picked up, not merely by the security forces, or the police, but by an enthusiastic radio ham who might report the matter. But they relied on the fact that they spoke in code, that their conversations were kept so brief

*from *The Springing of George Blake,* by Sean O'Bourke, Cassell, London, 1970.

Wormwood Scrubs

that it would be difficult to track down the sources either of transmission or reception.

But plans for rescue operations had to be changed. The various ploys adopted by O'Bourke and his associates were complicated and required careful briefing. For example, O'Bourke had to be told that the bars of a cell window were being cut and then stuck together again. There was going to be a break-out and it would be made on a rainy day which meant not only that O'Bourke must lie low on rainy days, but that if there was an escape security precautions in the prison would be stepped up.

Fortunately both Blake and O'Bourke took every precaution and did not attempt to evolve a detailed escape plan until every risk had been weighed up, every move timed to the nearest second. Yet it is still somewhat of a mystery why these conversations were not picked up, especially as Blake was a valuable agent whom the K.G.B. was known to be anxious to win back.

Every detail of the escape plan was worked out well in advance. Blake knew he would have a somewhat strenuous climb up and over the wall, using a rope-ladder and then to attempt a long jump. To get himself fit for all this he did Yoga exercises daily.

When the special inquiry team, headed by Lord Mountbatten, reported on the escape it was revealed that afterwards one of the cast-iron bars of a window was found broken. Around the broken bar was a strip of dark blue adhesive tape so the bar must have been broken either by Blake, or a confederate, well in advance of the springing.

O'Bourke tells of the final break: 'I got out of the car and got the rope ladder out of the boot. I looked up at the wall [of the prison], but it was too high. I stood on the roof of the car and threw the ladder and waited for Blake to ascend.'

It was a dark, wet Saturday night, with few people about, but Blake jumped badly and injured himself so that he had to be helped into the car. But O'Bourke got him safely away to a hiding-place in a rented room which was only a few streets away from Wormwood Scrubs. There Blake lay until the hue and cry was over after which he escaped to the Continent and on to Russia by a route the secret of which is still well kept.

Reference was made to what was then largely regarded as an escape aid only suitable for fiction writers in Lord Mountbatten's report. It was stated that two years before Blake made his successful escape the Governor of the prison had received inside information that 'a helicopter was to land in the yard behind the mail bag shop, pick up Blake . . . [and take him] to East Germany, either direct if the helicopter had sufficient range, or part of the way before he transferred to another aircraft if that was necessary.'

But, however like fiction rescue by helicopter may have

seemed then, this type of aircraft has in the last few years been successfully tried out as one of the latest and most effective of escape tools.

The first successful escape of this kind was from a Mexican jail in August, 1971. Joel Kaplan, reported to have worked for the American Central Intelligence Agency, and Carlos Castro escaped from Santa Marta Acatitla Prison, in Mexico City, when a helicopter lifted them out of the prison yard and took them to a waiting plane at a nearby field.

Even more dramatic was the helicopter snatch of Seamus Twomey, Kevin Mallon and Joe O'Hagan, three Provisional I.R.A. Leaders, in a daring, planned-to-the-last-second operation, when a masked gunman forced a helicopter pilot to land in an exercise yard at Mountjoy Prison, Dublin, on 31 October, 1973.

The helicopter, an Alouette Mark II, had been chartered from Irish Helicopters of Dublin three days before by a man with an American accent, calling himself 'Mr. Leonard.' He said he wanted to film Irish stately homes and monuments for a film company.

The pilot was told by 'Mr. Leonard' to fly to a lonely field in County Leix where he would pick up a film crew. When he landed there he was surrounded by masked men armed with rifles. Then, at gun-point, he was ordered to fly to Mountjoy Prison.

He landed in the prison yard where the prisoners were exercising and they were whisked promptly away to safety. Five minutes later the helicopter touched down at a disused race-course seven miles outside Dublin where cars were waiting. The escaped men jumped in and were driven off.

Technical aids to escape not only change from war to war, but also have to take into account the climatic conditions in the area where a war is being fought. For example, in the Korean War the American airmen were given what was known as an Escape, Evasion and Barter Kit. Its main purpose was to enable an escaping airman to bribe his way to safety if necessary. It comprised a watch, a ball-point pen (with compass), various trinkets which could be bargained for food, a revolver, ten dollars in cash and seven layers of clothing beneath the flying kit, wrap-around electric boots and fleece-lined winter boots, since those organising escapes from Korea soon learned that the exceptionally cold winters could be a bigger hazard for escapers than North Korean troops.

Chapter 11

Epics of prisoners-of-war

One of the most tenacious, obstinate and unconquerable of men to attempt to break out of prisoner-of-war camps in World War II was Douglas Bader, the Royal Air Force officer who had lost both his legs in a flying accident before the war and who, after repeated requests to the authorities was eventually readmitted to the RAF *as a flier* after war broke out.

Bader had been determined to make a come-back. He had not only mastered the use of artificial limbs – much more clumsy and difficult to adjust to in those days than now – but had even taught himself to play golf and to bat (though not to field) in an Old Boys' cricket match at his former school.

Getting re-accepted into the RAF, despite their desperate need for experienced pilots, was, however, far more difficult than he realised. But he won his way in the end, became a squadron-leader and led many sorties against the enemy with the fighter planes who won the 'Battle of Britain'.

Finally, after further promotion, he was shot down and captured by the enemy. The Germans, to their credit, were filled with admiration for Bader. They could hardly believe at first that a man without legs could also be a successful pilot. Maybe they thought that Britain had very few experienced pilots left, if she had to send legless men into action.

Nevertheless, they were compassionate. When Bader asked for another pair of artificial legs arrangements were actually made between the two warring countries, with Red Cross supervision, for the British to parachute a pair of limbs manufactured to the exact measurements to the enemy-occupied territory.

When, however, the Germans found that Bader really wanted these legs in order to be able to make an escape attempt and that the British needed him back because the return of such a hero would be a great boost to morale, they

Douglas Bader playing golf

145

Douglas Bader climbs into his plane for the Thanksgiving flight over London in 1945

were very angry indeed. Bader made a number of escapes, but was always recaptured.

The real epics of prisoner-of-war escapes often belonged as much to the men who stayed behind to organise them as to those who got away. Some stayed behind, not because they wished to, but because their organising ability and control over their fellow prisoners made them much more valuable helping others to get away.

One man who spent a great deal of the war helping Allied prisoners-of-war to escape and who in the end had to escape himself – on crutches! – was a cheerful, colourful character named Vladimir Bouryschkine, who, to avoid tongue-twisting difficulties in pronunciation, was nicknamed by the British 'Val Williams' after Valentine Williams, author of *The Man with the Club Foot*.

Williams, who was later officially recognised by MI9, though born in Moscow, had emigrated to the United States and was working for the American Red Cross at the time of the fall of France in 1940. He decided to stay on and as best he could help prisoners escape to England.

To this end he obtained the post of coach to a basketball team in Monaco and offered his services as a PT instructor to the Commandant of a prison camp, mentioning that under the Geneva Convention prisoners were entitled to half a day of PT each week.

This was the beginning of his recruitment as a key figure in the 'escape team' and which eventually brought him to London after he had organised the safe dispatch of a number of prisoners-of-war. In Britain Williams was trained in a special course for naval rescue teams. He was then parachuted into France to establish a base in Britanny, the idea being that he would set up hiding places for prisoners in Paris and then conduct them safely to a beach in Britanny from which the Royal Navy would take them away by night.

One of Williams' chief problems was that not only had some rescue units been 'blown' and destroyed by the Germans, but that in a few cases they had been infiltrated by enemy agents. It was hard to know who was friend or foe. Then, when he had assembled some ninety airmen in Britanny – all escaped prisoners – and was waiting at night with his friends on the beach at Le Palos-Plage, the dreaded radio signal came through – *'Denise est morte,'* which meant that London had cancelled the operation.

'As a result of this failure, Williams' situation had become dangerous,' wrote Airey Neave. 'At least ninety airmen had been collected in Britanny, of whom thirty-nine were hidden by the Comtesse de Mauduit. His only alternative, until a proper sea evacuation could be organised, was to take them through Spain.'*

This he attempted to do, but on the way was taken by the Gestapo and kept at Fresnes prison for a month. He could very easily have been executed as a spy, but somehow Williams bluffed the Germans into believing he was an RAF officer who had been shot down in a bomber aircraft and had decided to stay in France to join the Resistance.

By this means he was able to avoid being tortured into betraying vital secrets of escape routes. Eventually he escaped from Rennes prison, to which he had been transferred, on 20 December, 1943. A fellow prisoner had smuggled a minute saw to him in a bottle of wine, but at this first attempt to escape Williams was actually caught in the act of sawing through a bar in his cell.

Saturday at MI9, by Airey Neave, Hodder & Stoughton, 1969.

The next time he was luckier. He obtained a key, and, with the help of the same prisoner, got out of his cell and together the two men climbed down ladders left behind by workmen to the moat of the prison. When they got to the outer wall there was a long jump which Williams unhappily misjudged and broke a leg.

He hid in a hen-house with his fellow prisoner until dawn and undoubtedly would have been recaptured but for the fact that Williams had picked up an unusual piece of information in his escape training.

The German guards had taken out dogs to track down the escaping prisoners. Williams had learned that if, when dogs approached, one urinated, this caused the dogs to urinate, too, and consequently to lose the scent at the same time.

I cannot vouch for the absolute infallibility of this theory, but certainly it worked in the case of Val Williams and his

Val Williams and his fellow escaper take refuge in a hen house

comrade, and police-handlers of tracking dogs confirm that this act can seriously hinder locating hunted men.

The two escaped prisoners managed to get a farmer to drive them in his lorry under sacks of potatoes to a safe address where Williams had his leg put in plaster. It was on crutches that, with the greatest difficulty, Williams was taken to Paris. The final details of his escape were planned by one of MI9's most trusted agents, François Campinchi.

The latter arranged to have Williams 'arrested' by two French gendarmes who were in his pay and they escorted Val safely through the German control posts.

During the Korean War of the early 'fifties twenty-eight-years-old Captain Donald S. Thomas, a United States Air Force navigator-bombardier, had his twin-engine B-26 bomber hit by enemy gun-fire near Pyongyang, the North Korean capital. He pulled the handle to open the escape hatch for the pilot to climb out, but, when he attempted to follow him, found he was trapped in his seat.

With flames all around him Thomas began to think his end was near, but suddenly and unexpectedly he was hurled out of the plane and managed to open his parachute while he saw the B-26 crash into paddy fields.

His parachute caught in a tree, but he freed himself and dropped to the ground, discovering that in the process his right hand and wrist had been broken. Apart from this he was also suffering from severe burns and shock.

Thomas knew his burning plane would have been spotted by the North Korean communist troops and that they would come looking for him, so, weak as he was, he aimed to get as far away as was possible in his weak condition.

He knew that there were some North Korean Christians who secretly supported South Korea for which he, as a US

A B-29 flying over the mountains of Korea

airman, was fighting. His plan was to seek these out and hope that he could persuade them to help him. After many adventures, dodging the North Korean troops, crawling along in the shelter of ditches alongside the paddy fields, he eventually came across some friendly Koreans but only just before he was about to stop outside the house of an old woman who was a communist agent.

The friendly Koreans told him to hide under an upturned boat on the beach until it was dark. Late that night one of them returned, rapped on the hull of the boat and Thomas crawled out. He was conducted first to the North Korean's humble home, then he was hidden in a series of caves for some days. Enemy soldiers were still out looking for him, as they had seen him parachuting to the ground. The first caves were hastily dug out of the earth and could easily have been spotted by observant soldiers if they happened to pass that way. But in the meantime the band of Korean helpers worked

Korean women threshing grain, oblivious to the presence of military observers

feverishly on constructing an artificial cave which would afford greater protection.

The new cave was some distance from the village and Donald Thomas had to be carried there during the hours of darkness. He was still weak and had a bad cough as well. However there was some consolation in the fact that the Koreans had made a much better cave than the other two. It had straw-matted walls, a board ceiling and a trap-door entrance. It was so very nearly air-tight that Thomas more than once felt faint and had to prop the trap-door open slightly with a stick to get some air.

For seven days he had to exist largely on wheat mixed with water. Later he was moved to a fourth and a fifth cave. Probably his helpers watched where the soldiers searched for him and then built new caves in those areas when the troops had moved on.

Altogether Captain Thomas existed underground for more

than two months. He felt much stronger and became impatient to get away. Eventually a plan was worked out for Thomas to be taken out to sea in a small boat in the hope that he could come across a United Nations patrol ship which would rescue him. His idea was that they should head south towards Inchon, a friendly port, but the Koreans thought there was a better chance of a swift rescue by heading north towards Sinanju which UN ships had been known to shell regularly.

'Much more chance friendly ships up north,' said the leader of the party.

After a few days there was still no sign of any friendly Navy ships, American or British, so they anchored off a tiny island while the Koreans went ashore to get water from a spring and to catch roosting sea gulls which they cooked. The quest seemed hopeless until they came across a large junk whose owner agreed to take the whole party aboard and in return for the sum of ten dollars which Thomas had been saving up for just such an emergency since he crashed, promised to head towards Inchon.

Finally Thomas, together with his helpers, was rescued by a British destroyer, HMS *Cockade* – 83 days after his plane had crashed.

The Tombs prison house, as it was in the 1890s

Chapter 12

The longest and the biggest: records and mysteries

It is probably impossible to point with exactitude to the longest escape of all time, but if one examines the records of re-captured prisoners, then one of the candidates for staying free longest must be Leonard T. Fristoe, who escaped from Nevada State Prison in the USA on 15 December, 1923, and remained free until his son handed him over to the police on 15 November, 1969. Fristoe had been jailed for killing two sheriff's deputies in 1920 and, despite an intensive hunt for him he remained free under the name of Claude R. Willis for 46 years.

Probably the most sensational escape against all the odds was that of Dennis Sullivan in 1879. While actually waiting in the prisoner's dock in the Tombs (New York) police court in 1879, Sullivan suddenly vaulted over the railings, dashed to the open window and leaped through to the street below, despite the fact that there were numerous policemen in the court-room, one within four feet of the window. Twenty police set off immediately in pursuit, but Sullivan was never caught.

There are, of course, still many prisoners who not only escape, but remain free for years. Even in Britain, a relatively small island from which escape is not easy, between 1964 and 1965 of 81 jailbreakers only 32 were caught within that period. Only seven of the 32 were free for more than three months, it is true, but 16 had been free for the whole period.

The man 'on the run' the longest in Britain is John Patrick Hannan, an Irishman who escaped from the Verne Prison at Portland in Dorset on 22 December, 1955, and is still at large. He had only served one month of a 21-month sentence for assaulting two policemen and car theft when he escaped.

One does not often find a hero among the criminal classes, but Johnny Ramensky was one of the exceptions, as well as being one of the most spectacular escapers of the century.

Johnny Ramensky recaptured after his dramatic escape from Peterhead Prison, Aberdeen

Johnny, born of Lithuanian parents in Scotland, was 66 when he died, yet he had spent most of his life in prison. Indeed, if one added up all his jail sentences they would have totalled more than 50 years. He first hit the headlines when he dashed from the recreation hall of Barlinnie Prison with warders chasing after him. He climbed a drain-pipe and gave an exhibition of gymnastics on the roof before finally getting away.

In 1934 he made his first break from Peterhead Prison, Aberdeen, and stayed free for 30 hours before being caught. He climbed over the prison roof and eluded police guarding a nearby bridge by clambering hand over hand under the parapet. The guards were only a few inches above his head while he was making this perilous getaway: one slip on the snow-covered ledges would have been fatal.

Freed in 1942, with his country at war, he wanted to do

something to help. He was taken up to London to meet Brigadier-General Laycock, chief of Combined Operations. As a result of that interview Johnny became a Commando and, adopting the name of Ramsay, the British Army's most skilled instructor in the correct method of blowing safes. All his expert knowledge was put at the disposal of the British Army for use against the enemy.

He was trained in parachute-jumping – one of the oldest men to volunteer for this – and was dropped behind the enemy lines. In Italy he worked with the guerrillas and repeatedly risked his neck by prowling around German and Italian headquarters, breaking into strongrooms and blowing security safes.

He left the Army after the war, not merely a hero, but with a personal letter from Brigadier-General Laycock, thanking him for his 'gallant service'. But, as Johnny confessed long afterwards, 'I had the finest chance of going straight that ever came the way of a crook. But I didn't take it. For four years in the army I had left crime strictly alone . . . in May, 1947, I was caught inside a big store in York with a safe already primed for blowing'.

From then until his death in November, 1972, Johnny was in and out of prison, but still escaping. On three other occasions he got away for brief periods, but though he died in hospital he was sent there from Perth Prison.

One of the longest escapes of famous men and one which still captures the imagination in song, legend and films, is that of Prince Charles Edward Louis Philippe Casimir Stuart, known to historians as the 'Young Pretender' and to others as 'Bonnie Prince Charlie'.

With the whole of the English army hunting for him, 'Bonnie Prince Charlie' was on the run from 16 April, 1746, after the total defeat of his forces at the Battle of Culloden Moor, until 20 September that same year.

He had believed that with help from the French and backing from the clans in the Highlands of Scotland he could win back the British throne which had been denied to the Stuarts since the abdication of James II. At first he was sensationally successful. He won all his early battles in Scotland, marched into England and actually reached Derby. Yet at the very moment when victory was within his grasp and London was in a state of panic, some of his generals deserted him and advised a retreat to the Highlands. The retreat was fatal because the English immediately pursued and defeated his followers.

When he escaped from the battlefield at Culloden there was a price of £30,000 on his head. It was an enormous sum to offer in those days and the amazing thing is that though so many of the Highlanders were poor not a single one of them gave him away. At risk to themselves and their families they hid, fed and clothed him.

Although in modern times there have been attempts to denigrate his character the truth is that the personality of Prince Charles was his greatest asset in escaping. The ordinary people admired a prince of whom it was said that he 'could eat a dry crust, sleep on peas-straw, take his dinner in four minutes and win a battle in five'.

There were several anxious weeks moving from cottage to barn and learning to talk, dress and look like a Highlander before he achieved his first objective which was to escape from the Scottish mainland by boat to the Outer Hebrides.

It was often the common people who saved him from the clan leaders and aristocracy. When he came across a seventy-years-old tenant farmer and asked to be guided to Sir Alexander MacDonald and the Laird of MacLeod, the small tenant, Donald MacLeod replied: 'Does not your Excellency know that these men have played the rogue to you altogether and you mauna trust them?'

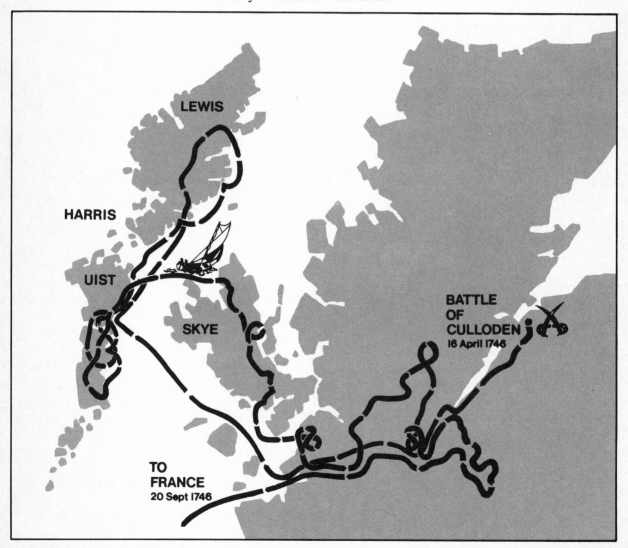

It was Donald MacLeod who found the Prince an eight-oared boat to take him away not only from the searching English soldiers, but from some of the more treacherous of the clan leaders. They sailed in a violent gale and because of this had to make a roundabout voyage, skirting the islands of Eigg, Rum and Canna before eventually they reached South Uist.

For the next month or two Prince Charles was forced to move from island to island in the Outer Hebrides to avoid detection, travelling to North Uist and Lewis and Harris only to find that the search for him had been extended to the remoter islands. Prince Charles dared not risk approaching any houses (all of them were watched) and he had to hide among rocks on the seashore, drenched in rain and desperately hungry.

It was then that the now legendary figure of Flora (her real Scottish name was Fionoghal) MacDonald came to his rescue. At great risk to herself this twenty-four-year-old girl became

Bonnie Prince Charlie

one of the vital links in the whole chain of chance acquaintanceships by which the Prince made his escape.

On the night of 21 June, 1746, the Prince walked over the moor to Ormaclett on the west side of South Uist where Flora was looking after her brother's cattle. She gave him food and shelter and it was then suggested that if she wanted to help the Prince to escape the best plan was for her to take him, disguised as her female servant, to the Isle of Skye.

Flora was originally somewhat reluctant to be drawn into all this but finally she agreed to bring a dress for the Prince to wear under the pretence that he was her maid, Betty. The militia suspected that Prince Charles was either in South Uist or the island of Benbecula, and slowly they converged on all sides of him. It was only through the ruse of posing as Flora's maid that he was able to get away to Skye under their very noses.

It is recorded that Charles had frequently to be corrected by Flora for the manner in which he played the part of her maid. She complained that too often he took 'great strides . . . and managed his skirts badly, holding them too high when he crossed over puddles in the road'. Yet the Prince himself maintained the spirits of the party when they went by boat to Skye, singing to keep them all cheerful.

They sailed into Loch Snizort in the Isle of Skye and landed safely after a narrow escape from an assault by the watchful militia. Then after working his way from north to south across Skye the Prince changed back again into male clothing and his farewell words to Flora MacDonald were: 'For all that has happened, Madam, I hope we shall meet in St. James's [Palace] yet.'

But they never met again and, though the Prince eventually escaped by boat to France on 20 September, 1746, from the very point in Scotland where he had landed 14 months earlier, this was the end of his campaign to win the throne.

As to Flora MacDonald she, together with others, was arrested and questioned, but because of lack of evidence against her was set free, though she spent some time in the Tower of London. She returned to Scotland where she had already become a legendary hero, married and died in the Highlands which she loved.

Traditionally, the most difficult place in the world from which to escape was said to be the French convict prison of Devil's Island off the coast of French Guiana, which acquired the reputation of being the world's most dreaded jail.
Not only did few escape from this closely guarded prison, but few lived to the date of their release. It is estimated that only about 2,000 of the 70,000 convicts sent there ever returned.

The most remarkable and thrilling story of an escape from Devil's Island is undoubtedly that of *Papillon,* the nickname given to Henri Charrière who wrote a book about his adventures, and caused a literary sensation.

Charrière was born in 1906 in the South of France. He went to Paris and became a criminal. He was charged with murdering another criminal – an offence which he always denied – and was sentenced to transportation for life to the penal settlement in French Guiana at the age of 25. He swore he would not serve his full sentence.

Henrie Charrière (Papillon)

Charrière's break after 42 days was made in an open boat and he covered more than a thousand miles and was befriended by an Indian tribe before he was recaptured. Returned to French Guiana and confined in Devil's Island he could meditate in 1941 that 'I'd been in prison 11 years, I was 35. I'd spent the best years of my life either in a cell or in a black hole. I'd only had seven months of freedom with my Indian tribe'.

After his early escapes he was put in solitary confinement in a cell only 10 feet high, with no opening whatever in its walls except for a small iron door with a little trap to it. He remained in almost total darkness with rats and centipedes nine inches long crawling around him. He was not even allowed to speak to the duty warder.

Yet – again by sheer power of personality – Charrière managed to have messages from confederates pushed under his door by the sweeper. Finally he made his break when he

Patients with self-inflicted wounds in the Devil's Island infirmary

took to the open sea, supported by only two floating sacks of coconuts. In the course of 13 years this determined man claimed that he made nine attempts to get away before he finally escaped.

When he reached Venezuela they allowed him to become one of their own citizens and he bought a schoolboy's exercise book and in two days filled them with the story of his escapes. He bought 11 more such books and in a couple of months they, too, were filled.

Charrière died on 29 July, 1973, but not before he had written one more book in which he described his adventures after he escaped. Perhaps then one must put a question mark against some of *Papillon's* claims such as his bid to tunnel under a bank and to bomb the Miraflores presidential palace. But there is no doubt he has become one of the great escapers of all time.

Papillon's escape story is much less a mystery than many. But, as escapes are usually carried out in great secrecy, it is not surprising that some of the most fascinating of them remain mysteries. There is the case of the enigmatic Count Alessandro Cagliostro of Sicily who made a reputation for providing 'magical cures' and selling his 'elixir of life' as well as being a remarkable prophet.

In the eighteenth century he was hauled before the Inquisition following an anonymous letter sent to the Paris police. Altogether he spent 18 months in the Bastille (the chief prison in Paris), but because no adequate evidence against him could be found he was released.

A contemporary engraving of Cagliostro

Later he was re-arrested in Rome on what was then regarded as one of the worst crimes of all – belonging to the Freemasons. For three of the remaining years of his life Cagliostro was confined in a windowless cellar without light or sanitation, food being let down to him through a trap-door in the ceiling.

Then in 1797 the French invaded the Papal States and the fortress of San Leo, to which Cagliostro had been transferred. They were told that the Count had 'just died'.

But had he? One story is that he escaped from his prison in 1795, took refuge in Russia and lived for a while in the home of Madame Blavatsky's father where 'in the midst of winter he produced by magical power a plate full of fresh strawberries for a sick person who was craving for it'.

Madame Blavatsky became founder of the Theosophical Society and was herself something of an authority on the occult. Did she learn all this from Cagliostro?

Nobody knows for sure. What is certain is that there was no positive proof of the burial of the Count and the feeling of the French investigators was that the men who had imprisoned him were lying and that in some way he had managed to get away.

There was the Reverend Philip St. John Wilson Ross, a clergyman who would appear to be an unlikely candidate to want to 'escape' from anything. A few years after World War II he decided he wanted to get away to start a new life on the continent of Europe with another woman with whom he had fallen in love.

One day he announced he was going to have a bathe and he went down to the seashore of the remote Welsh resort where he was staying, left his suit behind on the beach, with appropriate letters and documents in the pockets by which he could be identified.

He then put on a bathing costume, went into the sea, leisurely swam some distance to a lonely beach, and was picked up by car to be driven to his lady love.

The clergyman made his way to Switzerland under a false passport. But he had made sure that his wife and family were made financially secure by having taken out insurance policies on his life in their favour. Eventually his wife was given permission for him to be 'presumed dead through drowning', even though no body was found, and she was given the money.

He was ultimately discovered and returned to Britain. But the only charge which could be brought against him was that of using a false passport: he had not benefited under the insurance policies, nor made a claim for payment, so nothing could be done about that. Nor could the insurance money be taken from his wife.

Swimming off to a new life

Escape, or disappearance by faked drowning, is a technique that has been used down the ages and is, perhaps, one of the most fool-proof methods of escaping providing no body is discovered. Or, shall we say, providing any body that is discovered is assumed to be that of the escaper. Sometimes greater credence is lent to this type of escape by leaving a 'suicide note' behind. But as this method of escape is fairly common, it increasingly needs careful planning, as the police, who have to investigate all these matters, are always on the look-out for a staged disappearance.

Has he, or she, been depressed lately? Has there been treatment for depression by a doctor? Is there any reason for committing suicide? If there are no satisfactory answers to these questions, a 'suicide letter' may be treated with some suspicion.

It is not nearly so easy today to escape from one's job, home and normal surroundings without trace as it was a century ago. To grow a beard, or to shave one off is not enough; a wig, a surgical operation on the face, and other sophisticated disguises may be vital.

To escape successfully is very often to cover one's tracks so completely that the actual escape remains a mystery forever.

Thus some escapes will look like deaths and others will seem like fantasies thought up by romantic novelists. Take the story, for years accepted as historical fact, that the last Czar of Russia and all his family were butchered to death in a cellar at Ekaterinburg by Bolshevik revolutionaries in July, 1918.

For more than 50 years this was unhesitatingly believed by historians and statesmen alike. The odds still are that the Russian royal family were all killed, but what is now at last clear is that the inquiry into the whole affair by Judge Sokolov, the man chosen by the Czarist Russians to seek out the truth, was to a large extent based on false evidence concocted solely to discredit the Bolsheviks.

Whatever happened to them remains a mystery. No corpses were found, all evidence on the executions turned out to be secondhand or mere hearsay. Judge Sokolov's findings were based on the discovery in an old mine-shaft containing the Imperial Family's jewels (they could have been planted there), a human finger, which Sokolov asserted belonged to the Czarina, and a mass of bones.

The finger was discovered 10 months after the alleged executions, yet a photograph of it suggests it must have belonged to somebody who died days rather than months previously. As to the bones, a British forensic expert, the late Professor Camps, declared a few years ago that they were 'chopped up and were not positively human and could have been animal bones'. Further he insisted that no human skulls were found and that the bones did not add up to enough to account for eleven corpses.

Since then evidence has emerged of details of a plan to rescue the Czar and his family. The British, Americans and Japanese were all involved in it on a Secret Service level, even though their governments may have pretended otherwise. There was a plan for a fast motor-boat to take them away if the royal family could be smuggled safely to the north-west coast of Russia. There was also an American plan to take them across Russia to the south-east and Odessa and from there for a naval ship to bring them to safety in Malta.

Did the Czar and his family, or at least some of them escape? This is a modern theory that seems highly improbable and yet in recent years has been put forward with a good deal

The Imperial family

The Czar and his family at Tobolsk, where they were interned

The room in which the Czar and his family were supposed to have been murdered in Ekaterinburg, 1918

of evidence which may well have been forged. At least it keeps alive the faint possibility of an escape which, if it could be proved, would be the most sensational of modern times.

I have probed deeply into this whole affair and can only say, alas, that I very much doubt the success of any rescue attempt. I say this, despite the fact that I have seen coded messages purporting to come from American State Department archives which even announce the safe departure of the Czar and his family from Russia to Malta.

Not only this, but I have in my posession a specially designed book-matches pack with the title and photograph of the man who claims to be none other than the Czar's eldest son, who today holds court in the United States and expects to be accorded the title of 'Your Royal Highness' when addressed.

The mystery figure who claims to be the Czar's son is Lt.-Col. Mikhail Goleniewski, an officer of the Polish Intelligence Service, who defected to the Americans in West Berlin on Christmas Day, 1960. He brought with him a considerable amount of important information which resulted in the arrest of a number of spies.

He has even claimed to recognise a Mrs. Smith of Chicago as his sister, Anastasia. Those who have talked to him admit that he has a remarkable knowledge of the events of that tense period when the Czar and his family were under house arrest by the Bolsheviks.

But nobody has yet been able to confirm the validity of his claims, nor have they been able to prove the authenticity of the coded messages. So one must just write this down as the Great Unproved Escape of all Time.

It is when one gets close to the sphere of espionage that escapes become mysteries. In Milton (Hampshire) cemetery there is a grave which has a headstone bearing the words: 'In loving memory of my son, Commander Crabb. At rest at last'.

Ostensibly this is the grave of the brilliant Royal Navy frogman who on 19 April, 1956, volunteered for a special mission to dive into Portsmouth harbour secretly to inspect and explore the bottom of the Russian cruiser *Ordzhonikidze* which had brought the Soviet leaders, Marshal Bulganin and Nikita Khruschev to Britain.

His exploit was discovered by the Russians, Crabb disappeared and it was reported that either he was dead through a failure of his breathing equipment or because of action by Russian frogmen. Naturally when the story became public it raised a great scandal to the embarrassment of the British Government.

Then on 9 June, 1957, a fisherman saw a headless, decomposed body floating near a sandbank outside Chichester harbour, a few miles distant from Portsmouth.

Despite conflicting evidence the Coroner at the subsequent inquest declared that the body was that of Commander Lionel Crabb.

Did Crabb defect to the Russians? In other words when caught did he escape from his predicament by agreeing to work for the Soviet Union? This would not be an escape in the heroic tradition, but it may well have been his only way out. And did the British Secret Service, anxious to cover up the embarrassment of his having defected, concoct the story of the headless man as being that of Crabb?

Crabb's mother, now dead, merely said afterwards: 'They say it was the body of my son, and so I suppose I must believe them.' A few months later Mrs. Crabb was paid £100 by the Admiralty, but nobody knows what this was for. But the wording on the gravestone is odd: it smacks of officialdom and does not sound like what a loving mother would have put on the tomb of her son.

It is true that the Russians have never produced Crabb and announced his adherence to their cause. But two stories persist: one is that he had been ordered to let the Russians capture him and to pose as a defector to their cause, while still working for the British: the other is that the Russians had forced him on threat of death to join the Red Navy.

Crabb's girl friend in England has since received mysterious anonymous messages on the telephone, supposed to come from Crabb. 'He gave me facts and used a pet name which only Crabbie used,' she said. 'The message must have been genuine.'

Another curious thing is that *Pravda* and *Izvestia*, the Russian newspapers, published pictures of Crabb that must have been taken from his wallet. Then again Bernard Hutton, a Czech-born writer who has made a study of Soviet espionage, is convinced from evidence put before him that Crabb has been seen in Russia as a Red Navy lieutenant.

More damning than anything else is the suggestion that the Russians sent one of their agents to Britain to pose as an American Secret Service man to ask Crabb if he would make an under-water inspection of the cruiser, thus luring him into their hands.

Yes, escape means all kinds of different things to different people, as indeed we saw in the first chapter, and I think this final chapter underlines this point.

One must always remember that there are a thousand different ways of escaping and that in particularly difficult circumstances it may be the method of the seeming madman which is the only one which will work.

That is why I have included in this last chapter some of the unproved, mystery escapes. It is always possible that when the test comes you may find here an idea that will work when every other possibility seems doomed to fail.

Lieutenant Commander Crabb

Chapter 13

Lucky escapes

If ever a man faced odds of something like a million to one against survival it was John Lee at Exeter Jail on the morning of 15 November, 1884.

The scene was set for his execution. The public executioner, James Berry, had carried out his tests, set up the gallows, adjusted the rope and examined the trap-door through which the victim would drop. The prison bell had tolled and the chaplain had given the prisoner his last blessing.

John Lee had been sentenced to death for the murder of Emma Ann Whitehead Keyes, of Babbacombe, a Devonshire village in England, the previous November. There was some controversy as to whether Lee had really been guilty, but the circumstantial evidence against him was regarded as conclusive.

The picturesque village of Babbacombe today

The rope was adjusted round Lee's neck and the executioner moved back and pulled the lever to open the trap-door. It failed to work. He made an examination of the trap-door found all to be seemingly in working order and tried again. Still the trap-door did not budge. Poor Lee's agony continued, sweat pouring from his face as the executioner again tested the jammed trap-door.

'All is now correct. There should be no further trouble,' reported the worried executioner, as much to give some compassionate advice to his victim as to assuage the nagging fears which were causing him, too, to break out in a sweat.

For the third time he pulled the lever. Still the trap-door did not open. Seven minutes had passed since his first attempt to carry out the sentence and by now James Berry was as totally unnerved as John Lee. It was decided that whatever the defect was it could not be put right quickly.

This delay saved Lee's life. He became the only man in Britain ever to survive three attempts to hang him. And when the matter was referred to the Home Secretary, Sir William Harcourt, the latter humanely decided that Lee had suffered enough and commuted the sentence to life imprisonment.

It was, perhaps, one of the narrowest escapes from death which any man ever had. Eventually Lee was released from prison and he emigrated to the United States, married and lived until 1933.

Escapes, as we have seen, take many forms, and the narrow escape, the lucky escape and the fantastically bizarre, or almost occult escape, are in some ways the most fascinating. They have about them a quality of magic which is as dramatic as the stage managed 'escapes' of Houdini.

The tornado which struck Woodward, Oklahoma, in April, 1947, produced its own strange story. A chap called Bill was visiting his friend Al's house near Higgins, Texas, when the tornado went over them on its way to Woodward. Al heard the roar, went to the door to see what was happening and the door was snatched out of his hand and he was carried away over the tree-tops. Bill went out to see what had happened to Al and was himself lifted away 200 feet from the house. They were neither badly hurt, though Bill had somehow got himself tightly wrapped up in some loose wire, and they crawled back to the house. Only the floor was left intact. Al's wife and two children were huddled together on the divan, unhurt. One lamp was all that was left out of all their furniture.

Tornados, in fact, provide many instances of narrow escapes. There was the tornado of 1890 in Louisville, Kentucky, when the funnel never touched the ground, but roared across the city at 80 m.p.h., ripping off the upper storeys and killing 76 people but leaving those on the ground floors unscathed.

The formation of a tornado from ominous cloud to funnel

An outside chance enabled the identity of a badly shocked woman, whose memory had gone, to be established when in April, 1936, a minister in Cherokee, Alabama, found a photograph with her name on the back. He posted it back to her at Tupelo, sixty miles away, and later discovered that the tornado had struck the town and that she was in hospital with injuries and her five-year old daughter had been killed and her husband badly wounded. Her home had been torn to pieces. The photograph had been in a trunk which had been blown open and the picture carried away.

One of the narrowest escapes in history was that of the British Houses of Parliament on 5 November, 1605, a date that is still commemorated in many parts of England by Bonfire Processions and fireworks displays. True, this is the escape of an institution rather than an individual, but, had it succeeded, it might well have affected the lives of countless individuals for centuries to come.

It was a narrow escape in that it could so very easily have resulted in total disaster. Underneath the Houses of Parliament in London were many cellars which were let to merchants and other people who wished to store goods.

It was quite easy to organise the blowing up of the Parliament buildings by renting one of these cellars and filling it with gunpowder.

The Roman Catholics were angry with King James I, the Protestant son of a Catholic mother, for his indifference to their cause. They plotted to kill the King and all the leading Protestant statesmen and to put James's daughter Elizabeth on the throne and make Britain a Catholic country once again.

Their plan was to wait until Parliament was sitting and the King was present, and to blow them all up with gunpowder. Thirty-six barrels of gunpowder were carried into the cellars by the plotters, beside which sticks and firewood were piled, partly to hide the barrels, but also to fuel the fire once it had broken out.

Nobody had ever thought of patrolling the cellars and the plot went on for more than a year without being discovered. Guy Fawkes, the son of Protestant parents, who had been converted to Roman Catholicism, was chosen to carry out the plot. He was a brave man, because his task was to set fire to the gunpowder, and to escape if he could. His chances of escape were minimal.

But the plot failed because one of the plotters, named Francis Tresham, had a friend, a Roman Catholic peer, who would be among the Lords attending Parliament. Tresham did not want to see his friend die, so he wrote him a letter in disguised handwriting, and unsigned, warning him to 'have a care for your life . . . I advise you, if you love your life, to make some excuse so that you need not go to this Parliament. God and man are agreed to punish the wickedness of this time . . . Go away into the country where you may be safe.'

Tresham passed this letter on to Lord Salisbury who, in his turn, showed it to the King. There was a further phrase in the letter which both Salisbury and the King thought was sinisterly significant – 'they shall receive a terrible blow this Parliament.'

'A blow to Parliament?' inquired the King. 'That, surely, can only mean gunpowder being used to blow up the buildings.' So on 4 November, the day before Parliament was to meet, the cellars under the Houses were searched. There they found Guy Fawkes and the barrels of gunpowder.

Yet, but for Tresham's anonymous letter of warning, the plot would almost certainly have succeeded.

James I of England

THE HIGHE AND MIGHTIE PRINCE, Iames THE SIXT, BY THE GRACE OF GOD KINGE OF SCOTLANDE. R.E. fecit.

Admiral Lord Nelson

There are some people whose whole lives seem to be one narrow escape after another. This particularly applies to great men, whether they be generals, admirals or statesmen.

Nelson defied danger throughout his life as a sailor, both as midshipman and admiral. He lost an arm, the sight of an eye and suffered several near misses before he finally succumbed to a French sniper's bullet at the Battle of Trafalgar. He scorned safety and insisted on wearing all his badges of rank and medals in full sight of the enemy who, in those days, employed marksmen on their ships' masts to shoot down their opposing senior officers, if they could identify them. Nelson's answer to protests about his disregard for safety was that, if he was seen to be unafraid and defiant of the enemy, the men who served under him would be the same.

**Nelson's famous ship,
HMS Victory**

**An easy target for snipers.
General de Gaulle during
the war**

General de Gaulle equally had a charmed life. When he first entered Paris after the city's liberation from the Germans in 1944, his tall, easily recognisable figure, was a simple target for the few snipers the Germans had left behind. Similarly, even as an old man when he became President of France, he had two if not three narrow escapes from assassins. For at least three years of his presidency he lived in daily peril, for a secret organisation committed solely to killing him was operating inside France.

. . . and in peacetime

Winston Churchill, as we have already seen, had one lucky escape in the Boer War. Yet, like Nelson, he never heeded danger. All his life he defied the advice of his doctors, advisers, detectives and, on occasions, his King. Yet his narrowest escape from death was in many respects the most miraculous, even though it was the least spectacular.

On the night of 13 December, 1931, Winston Churchill stepped off the kerb on Fifth Avenue, New York, in front of Mario Constasino's taxicab. It may well be that he was so used to the driving on the left rule in Britain that he looked in the wrong direction when stepping off the kerb. Professor Lindeman, who later became Churchill's scientific adviser in World War II, made some mathematical calculations afterwards and decided that the blow Churchill received from the taxicab was '6,000 foot-pounds, equivalent to a fall of thirty feet by a man of Churchill's weight.'

As Churchill himself admitted later 'I ought to have been broken like an eggshell or smashed like a gooseberry.' He recovered remarkably quickly after a spell in hospital and he not only completely exonerated the taxicab driver and took the blame for the accident on himself, but visited the man's family and gave him a signed copy of his latest book.

Churchill was always mindful of the narrow escapes he had had: 'These hazards swoop on me out of a cloudless sky, and that I have hitherto come unscathed through them, while it fills my heart with thankfulness to God for His mercies, makes me wonder why I must be so often thrust to the brink and then withdrawn.'

Yet even more remarkable among narrow escapes are those when the near victim is rescued at the last moment by some inexplicable warning of danger. These incidents are far more prevalent than is generally thought: the most remarkable feature of them is that it is not as a rule the victim who is warned, but some other person.

For this type of narrow escape there are various definitions of the reason for it. Some say it is divine inspiration, others that it is pure coincidence, while those who keep a balance between these two views will probably say that it may have been extra-sensory perception a phenomenon which scientists cannot explain. ESP very often takes the form of an intuitive warning, or premonition.

Winston Churchill in 1931

Arthur Koestler, who wrote a book called *The Roots of Coincidence*, received a letter which gave an extraordinary story of a last minute warning that saved a man's life. In 1971 a young architect, who had suffered from a nervous breakdown, threw himself in front of a train in a London underground station and was taken to hospital. He was badly injured, but he recovered.

The gist of this letter was that the man's life was saved not because the train driver saw him and applied the brakes in time, but because 'quite independently, and with no knowledge of Harold, or of what he intended to do, some passenger on the train had pulled down the "Emergency" handle. And again independently of Harold's case, London Transport had interviewed this passenger with a view to

A London Transport Underground train

prosecution on the ground that he had no reasonable cause for pulling the handle.'

Yet the pulling of the emergency handle by the passenger saved the young architect's life. They had to jack up the train to get him out, so he must have been well underneath it. On the other hand a wheel cannot have passed over him, or he would have been killed. Pulling the 'Emergency' handle applies the brakes automatically, so he must have been saved from death by seconds. It should be stressed that it would be absolutely impossible for any passenger on the London underground railway to see what was happening in front of the engine.

What are we to make of this? Arthur Koestler, who has made a study of such cases, writes: 'If we assume that the unknown passenger acted on a telepathic impulse, we must also assume that it was a precognitive impulse, anticipating the event by a couple of seconds to stop the train in time. This is obviously a case which could be interpreted either in terms of telepathy combined with precognition, or as a "coincidental event".'

Are such cases coincidence, or are they the result of some telepathic communication? One could just say that the case quoted was a million-to-one coincidence. But I doubt if one could be quite so dogmatic about the story I am about to relate.

In the spring of 1944 a small ship of the British Royal Navy, travelling round the coast of Wales from Scotland, entered into a dense pall of mist. Suddenly, out of the blue, there came over on the inter-com the phrase 'Gor blimey, mate, pull up sharp, you're in real trouble,' spoken by an unknown voice.

Instinctively the commanding officer of the ship stopped engines. Almost immediately afterwards, coming like a note of doom, through the mist, was the ringing of a bell buoy: the ship was dangerously near rocks. Nobody pretended to understand about the 'Gor blimey' message: there was even a theory at the time that radio and even inter-com systems could pick up the conversations of London taxi-cab drivers. And, it was added, this lucky escape was entirely due to a coincidence.

But later that day another message was recorded on the inter-com: 'You have a sick man aboard your accompanying ship. Be sure you check. Land him at your next port.'

These mysterious warnings from an unknown source were followed out. The commanding officer of an accompanying ship was ill, though he was making light of his ailment. Only because the mysterious radio warning, never checked out, suggested he was seriously ill, was a doctor summoned when the ships reached Milford Haven. The diagnosis then was peritonitis. Without any doubt the warning saved the officer's life.

No amount of checking back helped to explain this warning. Not even the experts could explain how or why such messages should be received on the inter-com.

But, that narrow escape? It could be you or me, according to who cares most about our existence. Or, as most of us would put it, are you lucky or aren't you?

Acknowledgements:

Jacket designer: Len Embry
Artists supplies by Spectrum Artists Ltd.,
Michael Jackson, Robin Lawrie, Deryck Stenburg and
Ron Stenburg.

Special photography: Brian Long., Book designer: Len Embry.

The publishers would like to thank the following for their
help with illustrations.

Aberdeen Journals Ltd.
Associated Press Ltd.
BBC Copyright Photographies
The Bodley Head
Michael Brooker
British Film Institute
Camera Press Ltd.
Christopher Milbourne
Colorufic, Conway Picture Library
Frank Dagnall, Editions Orthaud
Paul Elek Ltd.
May Evans Picture Library
Illustrated London News
Keystone Press Agency
Maull and Fox Ltd.
National Portrait Gallery
Radio Times Hulton Picture Library
Scottish National Portrait Gallery
Spectrum Colour Library

The illustration on page 132 was reproduced from 117 Days
Adrift by Morris and Maralyn Bailey. Nautical Publishing
Co. Ltd.